新编英语九百句

课本

new English 900

First Printing--------April, 1978

published by

TAIPEI PUBLICATIONS TRADING CO

P. O. Box 59326 Taipei, Taiwan

Tel: 3618722

台　灣　版

發行人：黃　　　永　　　全

發行所：臺 北 圖 書 有 限 公 司

　　　　臺北市開封街一段六十六號407室

印刷所：文 大 印 刷 有 限 公 司

　　　　臺 北 市 萬 大 路 424 巷 16 號

新聞局出版登記局版臺業字第48號

中華民國六十七年 四 月　　日

定價 NT$

TP–076

new
English

book 3

Macmillan Publishing Co., Inc.
Collier Macmillan International
New York

Collier Macmillan Publishers
London

Taipei Publications Trading Co.
台北圖書有限公司

NEW ENGLISH 900

Project Editor: Peggy Intrator   **Contributing Editor:** Michael R. Lanzano

Senior Editor: Mary Ann Kingston Miller

Associate Editor: Gretchen Dowling

Consultant: Jean A. McConochie

Art Director: Zelda Haber

STAFF FOR STUDENT BOOK THREE

Editor: Ellen Shaw

Editorial Assistant: Elyn Raymon

Illustrator: Erica Merkling

Art Editor: Anna Sabin

Production Supervisor: Gerald Vogt

ISBN 0-02-974400

Collier Macmillan International, Inc.
866 Third Avenue, New York, New York 10022
Collier Macmillan Canada, Ltd.
Collier Macmillan Publishers
London

CONTENTS

Units 19, 20, 22-25 each contain two dialogue lessons and a bonus. Units 21 and 26 contain three reading lessons each. The main grammatical points featured are listed below.

INTRODUCTION

Welcome to English.

Welcome to New English 900®.
In this introduction, we want to tell you something about the books you are going to be using.

1. What is New English 900®?

NEW ENGLISH 900® is a six-level course for adult students of English as a second language. It contains material from beginning to advanced levels of study. The series consists of six student textbooks, six workbooks, six teacher's books, and reel-to-reel or cassette recordings.

2. An Updated and Revised Program

This series is a revision of the original ENGLISH 900® which takes its name from the 900 Base Sentences presented in the six textbooks. These sentences cover the basic structures and basic vocabulary of the English language. The **Base Sentences** of NEW ENGLISH 900® always appear in a complete and authentic context. They are presented in dialogue form as spoken by a cast of fully-drawn characters who use the English language in a natural way to communicate their thoughts, ideas, and feelings.

3. How Your Textbooks Are Organized

There are 150 Base Sentences in each book, and they are numbered consecutively from Base Sentence 1, Book

1, Unit 1, through Base Sentence 900 in Book 6, Unit 50. New structures are introduced in Base Sentences, and these sentences provide "building blocks" for the rest of the materials studied in the series.

a. The Dialogue Unit

There are ten units in Book 1. Each unit consists of three lessons and contains fifteen Base Sentences. In Book 1, every lesson opens with a short **Dialogue** containing the Base Sentences. As you progress through the series, a continuous and integrated story will be unfolded through the dialogues and, later, the readings. (However, each textbook can be used separately). The dialogues are followed by **Substitution Drills** that introduce variations of the Base Sentences and provide the student with the pronunciation and drill material needed for mastery. The **Exercises** in each lesson can be used as oral and written drills. In addition, every unit contains a **Grammatical Preview,** a **Refocus (review) Exercise,** and a **Bonus Dialogue.**

b. Reading and Refocus Units

Beginning with Book 2, each text contains two **Reading and Refocus Units.** These units consist of thirty Base Sentences introduced in three **Reading Passages.** They are followed by **Comprehension Questions** and **Exercises** that review and contrast aspects of the language previously introduced.

c. Intonation and Word Index

Other features of each textbook include a complete listing of the Base Sentences introduced in that book. This listing appears with **Intonation Lines.** In addition, there is a **Word Index** that lists, in alphabetical order, all the new words in the book, and notes the unit, lesson, and sentence in which each word first appeared.

4. Your Workbooks and Tapes

A companion **Workbook** is available for each of the six textbooks. The Workbooks reinforce material from the text and develop pronunciation and writing skills. They are designed to be used both at home and in the classroom.

A series of **Pre-recorded Tapes** has been prepared for language laboratory use. These tapes include all material from the Dialogues, Substitution Drills, Readings, and Comprehension Questions in the Student Books, and from the Pronunciation Exercises in the Workbooks.

5. The Teacher's Books

The **Teacher's Books** are an integral part of NEW ENG-LISH 900® Organized to correspond to the student text, the Teacher's Book offers techniques and strategies of practical value to the teacher in the classroom. Included are suggested lesson plans, cultural notes, and a step-by-step outline of ways to present and practice the new material.

Our Thanks

Based on many suggestions we have received from you, the users, we offer NEW ENGLISH 900®. It represents a careful and extensive revision of the widely popular original series. In it, we hope to have combined the best of the old with the most exciting of the new.

THE STORY SO FAR

In Books 1 and 2 we established the characters and plot of *New English 900*. We met **Bill O'Neill,** an ice cream salesman at the World's Fair, and through him we met **Laura Segura,** a secretary, and her boss, **Mr. Crawford.** Laura was not happy at her job and finally resigned. Mr. Crawford, the President of an advertising agency, is not happy about many things, including his son, **Michael.**

Through Bill, we met **Paulo** and **Joana Farias,** and their mother. Paulo is a manager at the Brazilian Pavilion at the Fair. His sister, Joana, is an art student. Their mother, **Alicia,** is visiting from Brazil. Joana and Michael Crawford met and began to think about each other.

The Nikzad family is from Iran. We met **Simon Nikzad,** a banker at the Fair, his wife, **Zahra,** and their sons, **Hussein** and **Ali.** Ali is lively, independent, and stubborn.

The O'Neill family is American. We met Bill's wife, **Nora,** and their four children: **Billy** (Bill, Jr.), **Jack, Peggy,** and **Suzy.** Nora decided to start a career.

Miguel Morales and **Pedro Ortega** are friends. Miguel, shy and quiet, is visiting from Colombia. Pedro is a ladies' man. Pedro and Miguel meet the girl upstairs, **Marta Garcia.** To Pedro's surprise, Marta prefers Miguel.

The Yamamotos own a store near the Fair. We met **Grandfather** and his grandson, **Jim.** We also got to know **Jim's mother and father.** Through the Yamamotos we see the changing values of the three generations.

These characters stay with the entire series and are the focus of our attention. An imaginary World's Fair provides a background for the series.

UNIT 19
I Need a Job!

LESSON 1

	LAURA:	Hi, Bill.
	BILL:	Hi, Laura. How are you today?
301	LAURA:	Awful. I resigned.
302	BILL:	You resigned? Why? You liked the job, didn't you?302
	LAURA:	Yes and no. I never liked my boss. You know that.
303	BILL:	Yes. But it was an interesting job, wasn't it?
304	LAURA:	Yes. We handled all the advertising and promotion for the Fair.
	BILL:	Well, what are you going to do now?
305	LAURA:	Find another job. Do you need a secretary? I type sixty words a minute.305
306/307	BILL:	[*laughing*] No, not today. But did you look in the newspaper?
	LAURA:	Yes. *Nobody* needs a secretary this week.

GRAMMATICAL PREVIEW

AFFIRMATIVE STATEMENTS

SIMPLE PAST
REGULAR VERBS

Subject
Pronouns   Verbs

I	danced	with Miguel.	
You	looked for	him.	
We			yesterday.
They	*cried	at the movies	
He/She	**stopped in	to say "hello."	

The simple past tense ending -ed has three different
pronunciations.

I cried   (-d)
I typed   (-t)
I needed   (-id)

It also has two different spellings: dance - danced
miss - missed

*Change the "y" to "i" and add "ed." cry → cried.. But, vowel + "y" adds "ed." Play
→ played.

**Some verbs double the last letter before you add "ed." stop → stopped.

NEGATIVE STATEMENTS

Subject Pronouns	(−) negative	Verb	(−) Contraction
I You We They He/She	didn't	play baseball yesterday.	did not = didn't

QUESTIONS

	Subject Pronouns	Verb
Did	I you we they he/she	play baseball yesterday?

Affirmative Statement: They played baseball yesterday.

Negative Statement: They *didn't* play baseball yesterday.

Negative Question: *Didn't* they play baseball yesterday?

Affirmative Question: *Did* they play baseball yesterday?

Answers: (a) Yes, they *did*.
(b) No, they *didn't*. They played football.

Tag Questions: (a) They played baseball yesterday, didn't they?
           (+)   (−)
(b) They didn't play baseball yesterday, did they?
           (−)   (+)

SUBSTITUTION DRILLS

1. I resigned from my job **this morning.**
today.
yesterday.
yesterday afternoon.
last night.
last week.
last Friday.

2. I **resigned from my job** this morning.
accepted a new position
asked for a raise
typed ten letters
tried to call you
stopped in to see you

3.   **We** handled the advertising and promotion for the Fair.
I
You
Our office
He
They
Two firms

4.   **Did** you *look in* the newspaper?
Didn't   *talk to* your lawyer?
show up at the meeting?
stop in at the employment office?
turn down a job last month?

5. You **liked the job,**   **didn't you?**
resigned,
filled out the form,
danced at the party,
watched a movie on T.V.,

6. You didn't resign,   did you?
               find another job,
               put an ad in the paper,
               buy that house,
               paint your apartment again.

7. It was an interesting job, wasn't it?
               exciting
               fascinating
               boring
               tiring

8. The job was interesting.
               exciting.
               fascinating.
               boring.
               tiring.

9. Do you need a new secretary?   —No, not today.
               want to buy a house?   this month.
               want to take a trip?   now.
                                                     right now.
                                                     until September.

CONNECTED DRILL

               type sixty words a minute.
                     run a mile   day.
               drink a quart of milk   day.
                  work forty hours   week.
                      earn $180   week.
                  take two days off   month.
       have three weeks' vacation   year.

EXERCISES

1. Change to the past. Follow the example.

Example: Laura types a lot of letters every day. (*yesterday*)
Laura typed a lot of letters yesterday.

a. Miguel listens to the radio every day. (*yesterday*)
b. She helps her mother every night. (*last night*)
c. Bill celebrates his birthday with his family every year. (*last year*)
d. Laura and Bill talk to each other every day. (*yesterday*)
e. They stop in at the office every morning. (*yesterday morning*)
f. The baby cries every night. (*last night*)
g. They play football every Saturday. (*last Saturday*)

2. Make negative statements. Follow the example.

Example: We watched a movie on T.V. last night.
We didn't watch a movie on T.V. last night.

a. Laura asked Mr. Crawford for a raise today.
b. He hired a new receptionist last week.
c. I walked to school yesterday.
d. Marta earned $200 a week last year.
e. We painted our apartment last month.
f. Pedro looked for a job this morning.
g. Michael tried to sell a painting the day before yesterday.

3. Make questions. Follow the example.

Example: They handled all the advertising and promotion.
Did they handle all the advertising and promotion?

a. He called up his girlfriend.
b. They walked to the Fair.
c. She baked a cake.
d. You ordered a dozen roses.
e. They danced all night.
f. I answered your questions.
g. It sounded like a bell.

4. Make affirmative or negative tag questions. Follow the example.

Example: Laura liked her job.
Laura liked her job, didn't she?

a. Bill wanted to help Laura.
b. You looked for my checkbook.
c. Mr. and Mrs. Crawford invited Joana to their dinner party.
d. I didn't insult you.
e. She didn't enjoy her vacation last year.
f. You turned off the air conditioner.

LESSON 2

308	BILL:	What about the employment office here at the Fair? Did you check with them?
309	LAURA:	No, I didn't.
310	BILL:	Why not?
	LAURA:	Because they aren't going to help me. I resigned from a good job!
	BILL:	Maybe you're wrong.
311	LAURA:	Oh, Bill. You need recommendations to get a good job. 311 Mr. Crawford isn't going to give me a recommendation.

312 BILL: Look. Mr. Crawford is difficult to work for, right?
LAURA: Right.
BILL: Well, maybe the employment office knows it, too.
313 LAURA: Is that possible?
314 BILL: Of course, it's possible! Maybe you're his seventh secretary in two years! **314**
LAURA: Maybe. Thanks, Bill.
315 BILL: Don't mention it. **315** Good luck.

SUBSTITUTION DRILLS

1. **Did** you *check with* the employment office?
   she *look in* the newspaper?
   he *call off* the meeting?
   you *pick up* your pay check?

2. **Didn't** Mr. Crawford fire Laura?
   you watch television last night?
   we cancel that meeting?
   I order lunch an hour ago?
   they work together yesterday?

3. **No,** he   **didn't.**
   I
   we
   you
   they

4. **You need** recommendations **to get a good job.**
   skills
   connections
   an education
   a neat appearance

5. Mr. Crawford is difficult to work for, **right?**
   isn't he?
   don't you think?

6. **Is that** possible?
   likely?
   true?

7. Thank you.   **—Don't mention it.**
   —You're welcome.
   —My pleasure.
   —Anytime.

CONNECTED DRILLS

1. Why didn't you **ask your boss?**
check with me first?
call me yesterday?
fill out this form?
fire her?
stop in to say hello?

—**Because** he doesn't listen to me.
I was in a hurry.
I didn't remember your number.
it was too long.
she needs the job.
we were busy all day.

2.   What **did you want**   yesterday? —To ask you
                                                                something.

Who	call	—My friend.
Where	stay	—At a hotel.
When	arrive	—At seven o'clock.
How many letters	type	—Thirty!
How much money	earn	—Fifty dollars.

3. You're his *seventh* secretary **in** two years!
This is my *first* cigarette   five days!
That was the *fourth* phone call   ten minutes!
This is her *first* vacation   three years!

EXERCISES

1. Complete this dialogue. Use the words below.

isn't • aren't • Did • didn't • not

BILL: What about the employment office here at the Fair?
_____ you check with them?
LAURA: No, I _____.
BILL: Why _____?
LAURA: Because they _____ going to help me. I resigned
from a good job!
BILL: Maybe you're wrong.
LAURA: Oh, Bill. You need recommendations to get a good job.
Mr. Crawford _____ going to give me a
recommendation.

2. Make questions and then answer them. Follow the examples.

Examples: 1. You learned a little more English yesterday. (*Yes*)
Student 1: *Did you learn a little more English*
yesterday?
Student 2: *Yes, I did.*

2. Laura didn't check with the employment office. (*No*)
Student 1: *Didn't Laura check with the employment*
office?
Student 2: *No, she didn't.*

a.   You watched a movie on television last night. (*Yes*)
b.   Mr. Crawford didn't fire his secretary. (*Yes*)
c.   Bill and Laura didn't walk to the employment office together.
(*No*)
d.   You and your brother stayed home last Saturday. (*No*)
e.   Laura didn't ask her boss for a raise. (*No*)
f.   I turned off the air conditioner. (*Yes*)

3. Make questions from these answers. Follow the example.

Example: She typed **a report.** (*What*)
What did she type?

a. The secretary asked her boss for **a few days off.** (*What*)
b. He fired **his accountant.** (**Who*)
c. Miguel lived in Colombia **two years ago.** (*When*)
d. You worked **until eight** last night. (*How long*)
e. Billy and Jack played football **in the park** yesterday. (*Where*)
f. She earned **$10,000** last year. (*How much/How much money*)
g. We repeated the exercise **ten times.** (*How many times*)

4. Make questions with "Why" and answer them with "Because."
Follow the example.

Example: Laura is unhappy. She resigned from her job.
Student 1: *Why is Laura unhappy?*
Student 2: *Because she resigned from her job.*

a. Mr. Crawford was difficult to work for. He is impatient.
b. You didn't stop in to say hello. I was in a hurry.
c. Billy and Jack didn't play baseball this afternoon. They studied all day.
d. Bill didn't come home on time. He stopped in at the flower shop.
e. Laura didn't like her job. She didn't like her boss.

See discussion in Book 5 Unit 36

BONUS DIALOGUE

MRS. CRAWFORD:	Hi, dear. How was your day?
MR. CRAWFORD:	Oh, the same.
MRS. CRAWFORD:	How's your secretary? Does she come in on time now?
MR. CRAWFORD:	Yes . . . well, in fact, she resigned today.
MRS. CRAWFORD:	Laura? Resigned? Why?
MR. CRAWFORD:	I don't know. Maybe because I criticized her typing.
MRS. CRAWFORD:	She's a good typist, isn't she?
MR. CRAWFORD:	Yes, usually.
MRS. CRAWFORD:	Well?
MR. CRAWFORD:	"Usually" isn't "always."
MRS. CRAWFORD:	You are too critical, dear.
MR. CRAWFORD:	Please. It's *my* business.
MRS. CRAWFORD:	Don't talk to me that way. And don't forget, it was my father's business. You're too critical of everything and everyone; of me, of the boys . . .
MR. CRAWFORD:	Jane, please, don't bother me.
MRS. CRAWFORD:	Look, Gary, I live here, too. They are my sons, too.
MR. CRAWFORD:	I'm tired, and I don't want to talk about it.

UNIT 20
All's Fair in Love and War

LESSON 1

	MIGUEL:	What a mess!
	PEDRO:	You sound like my mother.
		Watch out! Don't step on that sweater.
	MIGUEL:	Hey, that's *my* sweater.
	PEDRO:	Uh, yes, I guess it is.
	MIGUEL:	You're a slob, Pedro, but you're a great photographer.
316		Some of these pictures could be in magazines.316
	PEDRO:	Thanks, Miguel.
317	MIGUEL:	Hey, here's an old picture of you. You had a mustache!317
	PEDRO:	Let me see.
318	MIGUEL:	You're standing with a guy with long blond hair.
319		He looks American.
	PEDRO:	Yes, he is. He was my first good friend here. A very
320		creative guy. I met him at the art school downtown.320
	MIGUEL:	What's his name? You never talk about him.

SUBSTITUTION DRILLS

1. Some of these pictures could be **in magazines.**
in an exhibit.
in a photography show.
valuable.
worth a lot of money.

2. I had **a mustache.**
a beard.
long hair.
glasses.
braces on my teeth.

3. He looks **American.**
European.
Oriental.
rich.
confused.
tired.
sad.

4. In the picture,

| you're | **standing with** | a guy with long blond hair. |

> looking at
> talking to
> sitting next to
> shaking hands with

CONNECTED DRILL

| Where did you | **meet Michael?** |

> see me?
> run into Laura?
> take photography courses?
> buy that book?
> sell your pictures?

| **met him** | at the art school downtown. |

> saw you
> ran into her
> took them
> bought it
> sold them

EXERCISES

1. Complete these sentences. Use the words below

**met • took • ran into • saw • bought
had • sold**

a. Did he buy roses for his wife?
    —No, he didn't. He _____ tulips.

b. Did you have a good time at the Fair?
    —Yes, we did. We _____ a great time!

c. Did they sell their house?
    —Yes, they did. They _____ it and moved to Florida.

d. Did you meet my sister?
    —No, I didn't. I _____ your brother, but I didn't meet
    your sister.

e. Did she take a taxi to work this morning?
    —No, she didn't. She _____ a bus.

f. Did you see Laura today?
    —Yes, I did. I _____ her on my way home.

g. Did they see a movie last night?
    —Yes, they did. They _____ an old war movie.

2. Answer these questions. Follow the example.

Example: Where did you meet your husband? (*at a party*)
I met him at a party.

a. What did you have for dinner? (*a hamburger*)
b. When did you sell your car? (*last year*)
c. Where did you run into Bill? (*downtown*)
d. What did you buy your boyfriend for his birthday? (*an expensive tie*)
e. Where did you see the photography exhibition? (*at the museum*)
f. When did you take Spanish? (*two years ago*)

3. Change to "look" + adjective. Follow the example.

Examples: 1. They look like ***Americans.**
They look American.

2. It looks like an **expensive** car.
It looks expensive.

a. He looks like a **European.**
b. He looks like a very **creative** guy.
c. It looks like a **delicious** cake.
d. They look like **Canadians.**
e. She looks like an **interesting** person.

4. Change "maybe" to "could be." Follow the example.

Example: **Maybe** that man **is** European.
That man could be European.

a. **Maybe** this photograph **is** worth a lot of money.
b. **Maybe** tulips **are** too expensive this time of year.
c. **Maybe** the Chinese restaurant **is** crowded this time of day.
d. **Maybe** these books **are** valuable.
e. **Maybe** those people **are** buying tickets for the exhibition.

*American = American person. Be careful—adjectives and nouns of nationality are not always the same.

LESSON 2

321	PEDRO:	His name's Michael. He was in love with this woman. 321 He wanted to marry her. She was beautiful, but crazy.
	MIGUEL:	What do you mean "crazy?"
322	PEDRO:	One day, she came to my door. She didn't love
323		Michael anymore. 322 She fell in love with me. 323
324	MIGUEL:	Just like that?
325	PEDRO:	Well, sure, I flirted with her, but I flirt with everyone!
	MIGUEL:	What happened?
326	PEDRO:	You know I can't resist a pretty face.

	MIGUEL:	And Michael? What did he do?
327/328	PEDRO:	He never spoke to me again. About a year ago I tried to call him, but he hung up on me.
	MIGUEL:	What happened to the girl?
329	PEDRO:	We saw each other a few times. 329 Then she moved to Florida. She has a sister there.
330		Things like that don't last long. 330

SUBSTITUTION DRILLS

1. Michael was **in love with** this woman.
engaged to
married to
separated from
divorced from

2. He **wanted** to marry her.
planned
hoped
expected
decided

3. One day she **came to my class.**
ate dinner with me.
gave me a call.
hung up on me.
threw me out.

4. It happened **just like that?**
all of a sudden?

5. We **saw** each other **a few times.**
ran into   once.
spoke to   once or twice.
called   every now and then.
went out with   from time to time.
wrote to   a couple of times.

6. You know I can't resist **a pretty face.**
a nice figure.
a man with a beard.
a beautiful smile.
long hair.
redheads.

7. **Things like that** don't last a long time.
Business problems
Love affairs
School romances

CONNECTED DRILLS

1. She didn't **love Michael** anymore. She **loved me.**
   wear dresses   wore jeans.
   teach French   taught English.
   drive a big car   drove a small one

2. Well, sure, I **flirted** with her, but I **flirt** with everyone!
     spoke   speak
     went out   go out
     fell in love   fall in love

3. Didn't you ever **see**   him after that?
     say anything to
     think about
     dream about
     hear from
     write to

  —No, I never **saw**   him again.
     said anything to
     thought about
     dreamed about
     heard from
     wrote to

4. Did you ever **try to talk to him?**
    send her a letter?
    meet her parents?
    read anything about him?
    find her letter?

  —Yes. I **tried to call him** a year ago.
    sent her a card
    met them
    read an article about him
    found it in my desk

EXERCISES

1. Complete the sentences. Use the words below.

hung up • had • wrote • took • heard • married

a. Didn't Alice and Jim get _____?
   —No. They _____ a fight, and they don't see each other
   anymore.

b. Did Pedro call Michael?
   —Yes, but Michael _____ on him.

c. Did Miguel hear from his mother last week?
   —Yes, as a matter of fact, he _____ from her yesterday.
   She _____ him a nice long letter.

d. You're early. Did you run all the way here?
   —No. I _____ a bus.

2. Change to the present. Follow the example.

Example: Ali **had** ice cream **yesterday.**
Ali has ice cream every day.

a. Billy and Jack wore jeans yesterday.
b. Mrs. Farias wrote to her husband yesterday.
c. Pedro's room was a mess yesterday.
d. Bill saw Laura yesterday.
e. Miguel thought about Marta yesterday.
f. Our teacher taught us some new words yesterday.

3. Add "but" and talk about yesterday. Follow the example.

Example: We didn't see each other today.
We didn't see each other today, but we saw each other yesterday.

a. I didn't go out with her today.
b. They didn't eat lunch with us today.
c. We didn't speak with them today.
d. She didn't wear a hat today.
e. He didn't read the newspaper today.

4. Answer these questions. Follow the example.

Example: Did you buy blue paint or green paint? (*green*)
I bought green paint.

a. Did you drive to Florida alone or with someone? (*alone*)
b. Did you have one piece of apple pie or two? (*one*)
c. Did you come home at six o'clock or seven? (*six o'clock*)
d. Did you go to Korea last year or the year before last? (*the year before last*)
e. Did you give her a gold ring or a silver one? (*gold*)

BONUS DIALOGUE

BILL: Hi, Paulo.

PAULO: Hi, Bill. How's business?

BILL: Fine. How's yours?

PAULO: Coming along. We're opening some new exhibition soon. Oh, by the way, we're looking for a secretary.

BILL: Really? I know a good one. She wants a new job.

PAULO: Where can I find her?

BILL: I can give her your number. I see her every day.

PAULO: O.K. Here's my *card. Tell her to call me. Oh, what's her name?

BILL: Laura Segura.

PAULO: Segura . . . Isn't she Mr. Crawford's secretary?

BILL: She was. She resigned.

PAULO: I don't think I can hire her. My office does a lot of work with Mr. Crawford's office. It could be embarrassing.

BILL: I see. That's too bad.

PAULO: Yes, it is. But perhaps we can find her a job in another department.

BILL: Thanks, Paulo.

PAULO: Sure, Bill.

*His business card.

Past Tenses of irregular verbs in this unit*

BASE FORM	PAST FORM
buy	bought
come	came
dream	dreamed/dreamt
drive	drove
eat	ate
fall	fell
find	found
get	got
give	gave
go	went
hang	hung
have	had
hear	heard
meet	met
read	**read
run	ran
say	said
see	saw
sell	sold
speak	spoke
take	took
teach	taught
think	thought
throw	threw
wear	wore
write	wrote

*There is a longer list of past forms of common irregular verbs at the end of this book.
**Pronounced "red."

UNIT 21
Reading and Refocus

LESSON 1

A Letter to Miguel's Mother

Dear Mama,

331   There is so much to tell you, Mama. 331 Everything here seems different, but, at the same time, everything seems the same. Yesterday was a good example.

332   At 7:00 the alarm clock rang and woke us up. 332 I turned on the radio, and we listened to the news. But the news is in English, not Spanish. For breakfast, we have coffee and bread, but the coffee and bread don't taste the same as they do at home. Even the water tastes different! 333 At 9:00 I left the house. 334

33/334

335   At night, after dinner, we talked and watched television. 335 The movies here are the same: war stories, westerns, and mysteries. At about 9:30 one of Pedro's friends stopped in to say hello. 336 At about 11:00 Pedro called each one of his twenty girlfriends to say good night and told each one a different story. 337 I like Pedro more and more. 338

336
337

338
339   I learn a little more English every day. Yesterday, I learned the word "embarrassed." 339

Love,

Miguel

340   P.S. You asked for a photograph. Here it is. The girl next to me is Marta. She lives upstairs. 340

Questions about "A Letter to Miguel's Mother"

Fact:
The answers are *clear* in the letter.

1. Is life in America the same as life in Colombia in some ways or is everything different?
2. Did Miguel listen to the news at seven a.m. yesterday?
3. Does Colombian coffee taste the same as or different from American coffee?
4. Does Miguel like Pedro?
5. What time did Miguel leave the house?
6. What time did Miguel wake up yesterday?

Inference:
You can *guess the right answers* from the letter.

1. Did Miguel listen to the news on the radio in Colombia?
2. Was the news in Spanish or in English in Colombia?
3. What does Miguel's family have for breakfast in Colombia?
4. Do they have war stories, westerns, and mysteries on television in Colombia?
5. Is Pedro always honest or does he sometimes lie?
6. How does Miguel feel about his visit to New York?

To the Student:
There are *no wrong answers* to these questions.

1. Do you have coffee and bread for breakfast?
2. Do you listen to the news on the radio, watch it on television, or read it in the newspaper?
3. After dinner, do you usually go out or stay home?
4. What television shows do you like to watch?
5. Do you like to learn about different countries?
6. What does "embarrassed" mean in your language?

USING YOUR ENGLISH

I. THE SIMPLE PAST TENSE

A.   Carole is an editor. She works at a large publishing company in
Boston. She has a very busy life. Each morning she gets up at 6:30.
She takes a shower and gets dressed. Then she has a roll and coffee.
She takes the bus to work. On the way to work she reads the
newspaper. At work she meets with authors and reads their work.
She goes home at 6:00.

B. This year Carole has a different job. Rewrite the paragraph in the
past tense. What did Carole do last year?

Begin with: *Last year Carole was an editor.*

C. Tell me about your day yesterday. Answer these questions.
1.   Did you go to work?
2.   Was it a busy day?
3.   What time did you get up?
4.   Did you eat breakfast? What did you have?
5.   Did you walk to work?
6.   Did you read anything on your way to work?
7.   What did you do at work?
8.   What time did you go home?

II. EVEN

A. *Even* can show surprise or emphasis.

B. Use *even* in these sentences.
1.   Everyone is sick, _____ the baby.
2.   The food in this restaurant is awful. _____ the water is
bad.
3.   Everyone cried at the movie, _____ John, and he *never*
cries.
4.   Mr. Tweed doesn't love his children.
    —That can't be true! _____ animals love their children.
5.   Your new apartment is beautiful. _____ the door is
beautiful!

III. TALK ABOUT TIME

A. AT -o'clock, noon, midnight, night
   IN   the morning, afternoon, evening
   IN   January, February, . . .
   IN   1978
   ON Monday, Tuesday, weekdays, weekends
   ON January 2nd, March 14th, the 20th (of any month)

B. Use *in, on,* or *at* in the spaces below.
   1. He doesn't work _____ Sunday.
   2. He was in Africa _____ 1964.
   3. He likes to sleep late _____ weekends.
   4. She goes out _____ night.
   5. We're leaving _____ July 1st.
   6. They are leaving _____ midnight.
   7. I go to work _____ 7:30 a.m.
   8. I am going on vacation _____ August.
   9. The party begins _____ about 9:30.
   10. We have a meeting _____ the first Monday of every
       month.
   11. We're getting married _____ Saturday, June 16th.
   12. We eat breakfast _____ 7:00 _____ the
       morning.
   13. The party is _____ 8:00 _____ the evening
       _____ Friday, May 3rd.
   14. The President is going to speak _____ 9:00
       _____ Thursday.
   15. I am seeing her _____ Sunday afternoon _____
       4:00.

IV. TELL and SAY*

A. *Tell* and *Say* are confusing because they refer to similar things.

1. Certain expressions always use *tell.*

Examples: a. *tell* a lie
b. *tell* a story
c. *tell* the truth
d. *tell* a secret
e. *tell* the time

2. Here are some uses of *say:*

Examples: a. He *said* good night to each one of his girlfriends.
b. They *say* she is shy.

3. *Note:* *Say* and *tell* with the indirect object.

a. With *tell* there are two possibilities.
1. She *tells* me a story before I go to sleep.
2. She *tells* a story *to me* before I go to sleep.

b. With *say* there is only one possibility.
He always says good night *to me.*

B. Use the correct form of *say* and *tell* (in the present) in the sentences below.
1. He _____ his children stories every night.
2. They _____ he is rich.
3. Don't _____ lies.
4. The boss always _____ good morning to me.
5. Do you always _____ the truth?
6. Can you _____ me the time?
7. You can _____ me. I never _____ secrets.
8. He always _____ hello to you in his letters.

*These are not the *only* uses. We discuss indirect speech with *say* and *tell* in Book 6.

LESSON 2

Laura's Story

341   My father died the year I was born.₃₄₁ Life was difficult in Spain in those years. My mother decided to move to Mexico because people said things were easier there. And there was

342 no reason to stay in Barcelona. It broke my mother's heart to

343 leave, but it also broke her heart to stay.₃₄₂ She sold her diamond ring, the only thing she had, and bought two tickets to Mexico.₃₄₃

344   There, in Mexico, I forgot yesterday's miseries. After all, I

345 was only a child.₃₄₄ But our new life was not like my

346 mother's golden dreams.₃₄₅ I grew up and had to go to work.₃₄₆ I was very unhappy. We were poor and alone in the world.

347   At eighteen, I married an older man. He had a little

348 money, and I spent a few happy years with him.₃₄₇ I got

349 new clothes and lived in a fine house.₃₄₈ But I didn't love him, and I think he knew it, too.₃₄₉ It wasn't his fault. He wasn't a bad husband. He wanted a quiet life and a big

350 family. I didn't. We fought about it and made each other miserable.₃₅₀ Finally we got a divorce. After that I came to New York.

Questions about "Laura's Story"

Fact:
The answers are *clear* in the story.

1. Where was Laura born?
2. Why did Laura's mother decide to move to Mexico?
3. Did Laura grow up in Mexico or in Spain?
4. Was life as happy as Laura's mother's golden dreams?
5. Did Laura marry an older man or a man her age?
6. Did Laura love her husband?

Inference:
You can *guess the right answers* from the story.

1. Was Laura's mother happy or unhappy with her life?
2. Did Laura and her mother want to change their lives?
3. What did Laura do to change her life?
4. Why did Laura and her husband get a divorce?
5. Was Laura just looking for an easy life, or was she looking for love, too?
6. Wasn't Laura a little like her mother in some ways?

To the Student:
There are *no wrong answers* to these questions.

1. Why do you think Laura married an older man?
2. Do you think Laura's life in New York is happier or less happy than in Mexico?
3. At what age do most women get married in your country?
4. Do many people get divorced in your country?
5. Was your childhood easy or difficult?
6. Do you want to be in the same city in five years?

USING YOUR ENGLISH

I. A FEW, NOT MANY, A LITTLE, NOT MUCH, A LOT OF

A. Look at these sentences:

1. a. Michael likes to talk on the phone. He makes *a few* calls every night.
   b. Peggy doesn't like to talk on the phone. She does*n't* make *many* phone calls.

2. a. Ellen has *a little* money in the bank. She's going to get a car.
   b. Barbara does*n't* have *much* money. She can't pay her rent.

B. Both *a few* and *a little* mean a small quantity, but the emphasis is positive. We use *not many* and *not much* to give a negative emphasis.

A FEW(+) NOT MANY(−) A LOT OF(+) MANY(+)	}	CALLS	A LITTLE(+) NOT MUCH(−) A LOT OF(+) }	MONEY

We use *a lot of* in both cases to show a large quantity. We don't usually use *much* in an affirmative sentence.

Examples: 1. *Many*
                   A lot of } people live in New Delhi.
              2. Venezuela produces *a lot of* oil.

C. Complete the sentences as in the examples. Use *a little, not much, a few,* or *not many.*

Examples: 1. They _____ money in the bank, and they are going to buy some furniture. (*have*)
They have a little money in the bank, and they are going to buy some furniture.

2. They _____ money in the bank, and they can't afford to buy any furniture. (*have*)
They don't have much money in the bank, and they can't afford to buy any furniture.

1.   We don't have a large garden, and we _____ flowers for the table. (*have*)
2.   We don't have a large garden, but we _____ flowers for the table. (*have*)
3.   It's a small fire, and it _____ heat. (*give*)
4.   It's a small fire, but it _____ heat. (*give*)
5.   It's hard to find work these days. There _____ jobs. (*be*)
6.   I'm lonely. I _____ people here. (*know*)
7.   I _____ bread because I'm on a diet. (*eat*)

8.   The professor is very busy, but he usually _____ time for his students. (*have*)
9.   There _____ apples in the box. We can't make a pie. (*be*)
10.   There _____ apples in the box. We can make a pie. (*be*)

II. BE BORN

    A. 1. I *was born* in Spain. (He, She, It)
       2. You *were born* in 1936. (We, They)

B. Use *was born* and *were born* in the sentences below.
1. We _____ in the United States.
2. I _____ in 1940.
3. Mr. Rich _____ *with a silver spoon in his mouth.
4. My sisters _____ in the same hospital.
5. Sometimes I think I _____ in the wrong century.
6. What sign of the zodiac _____ you _____ under?
7. What year _____ he _____?
8. _____ you _____ in the same country as your
    parents?

III. GET

    A. The verb *get* has many meanings. In Book 2, Jim said, "Mr.
       Yamamoto never *gets* angry."
       In that sentence *get* means "become."
       Another meaning of *get* is "obtain."

Examples: 1. We *got* a divorce.
           2. I *am getting* some new clothes.

B. Use the correct form of "get" in the sentences below. Here,
    they all mean "obtain."
1. He _____ a raise every six months.
2. We always _____ the kids new toys for their birthdays.
3. I _____ a new suit last week.
4. I usually _____ a sandwich for lunch.
5. I'm _____ a pocketbook for my wife. It's her thirtieth
    birthday.
6. After college, I'm going to _____ a good job.

*" Born with a silver spoon in his mouth"–born into a rich family.

IV. APPOSITIVES

A. In the first two sentences "the only thing she had" and "her diamond ring" refer to the same thing. In the second two sentences "Suzanne" and "my sister" refer to the same person.

Examples: 1. She sold *the the only thing she had, her diamond ring*.
She sold *her diamond ring, the only thing she had*.

2. *My sister, Suzanne,* is going to college.
Suzanne, my sister, is going to college.

3. Follow the examples above and change the position of the appositives.

1. Mr. Crawford always carried his favorite gift, the pipe his father gave him.
2. John and Ellen, my first cousins, are studying medicine.
3. Ms. Extrator, my editor, works for a publishing house in Boston.
4. He was born on January 1, New Year's Day.
5. Mrs. Lancer, my teacher, is going to Brazil next year.
6. Mrs. Farias is writng a letter to her husband, Francisco.

LESSON 3

A Letter to Mr. Farias

My dear husband, Francisco,

I miss you, my dear, but we are happy and healthy, and the children send their love. Paulo is busy every minute. He is just like you, so sensible, maybe too sensible. 351 He thinks about business all the time. He doesn't have any real friends here.

Joana is growing up before my eyes. 352 Every day she grows more mature, less shy, and more confident. 353 She's getting serious about art again, so she's going to take some courses at one of the schools here. 354 She's talented, but not very patient. 355 She has a lot to learn.

I am enjoying the Fair, but most of all, I am enjoying the children. 356 I am very proud of them. At first, Joana was nervous about her English, but now she is almost fluent. 357 As a matter of fact, she is teaching me!

So, my dear, how are you? 358 How are things at home? 359 I miss you. I read and reread all your letters. 360

Your devoted wife,

Alicia

Questions about "A Letter to Mr. Farias"

Fact:
The answers are *clear* in the letter.

1. Does Mrs. Farias miss her husband?
2. Is Paulo very sensible?
3. What does Paulo think about most of the time?
4. Where is Joana going to take a course?
5. What is Mrs. Farias enjoying most, her children or the Fair?
6. Are Mrs. Farias's children making her happy or sad?

Inference:
You can *guess the right answers* from the letter.

1. Does Paulo often do things just for fun?
2. Why doesn't Paulo have many friends in New York?
3. Does Mrs. Farias think Paulo works too much?
4. Was Joana more confident or less confident two months ago?
5. Is Joana's English less fluent or more fluent than her mother's?
6. Why isn't Mr. Farias in New York with his family?

To the Student:
There are *no wrong answers* to these questions.

1. Why is Mrs. Farias proud of her children?
2. Did Mrs. Farias come to New York to see the Fair or to be with her children?
3. Are you the same person you were last year?
4. Are you more like Joana or Paulo?
5. Do you think someone can be too sensible?
6. Mrs. Farias signed her letter "your devoted wife." How do you sign your letters?

USING YOUR ENGLISH

I. Indirect Object Position

A. Look at these sentences. They mean the same thing.

1. Buy a shirt for *Paulo*.
   Buy *Paulo* a shirt.

2. Read the article *to him*.
   Read *him* the article.

B. Change the position of the indirect object in the sentences below.

Example: I'm going to buy that book for Ted.
I'm going to buy Ted that book.

1. Don't forget! Write a letter to me every week.
2. Our son gave a beautiful anniversary present to us.
3. I forgot my money. Can you lend five dollars to me?
4. I'm going to buy some art supplies for Joana.
5. I'm going to send post cards to you from London, Paris, Rome, and Tehran.

6. I don't have my glasses. Please read this article to me.
7. At the end of the school year, the teacher baked a cake for us.
8. Give my best regards to them.
9. Are you going out? Buy a pack of cigarettes for me, please.
10. Every night he tells a story to his children.

II. The Prefix *re-*

A. When you add *re-* to a verb, it means "again."

Example: Please *reread* this paragraph.
Please *read* this paragraph *again.*

You can't add it to all verbs, but here are a few.

1. Recopy this sentence.
2. Rewrite this paragraph.
3. Retype this letter.
4. Retell that story.

B. Rewrite the above sentences. Take out *re-* and add *again.* (Look at the example.)

III. JUST

A. Sometimes *just* means *exactly*.

Example: He looks like you.
He looks just like you.

B. Add the word *just* to these sentences. Follow the example.
1. This wine tastes like vinegar.
2. The table is the right size for their kitchen.

3. Your dress looks like mine.
4. You sound like my mother.
5. This tie is the right color for your shirt.

IV. SO

A. One of the meanings of *so* is "therefore." It connects a cause with a result.

Example: She's getting serious about art again. She's going to take some courses...

She's getting serious about art again, so she's going to take some courses.

B. Pick a sentence from column 1 and combine it with a sentence from column 2. Use *so*.

1	CAUSE
1.	I'm sick.
2.	I'm hungry?
3.	I don't have any money.
4.	My shirt is dirty.
5.	I'm going to work in France.

2	RESULT
	I can't buy my friend a present.
	I can't wear it this evening.
	I'm going to eat dinner early.
	I have to learn French.
	I'm not going to work today.

C. We also often use *so* in conversation or informal writing to connect a new thought to the previous thoughts.

Example: *So, my dear, how are you?*

Use *so* in the sentences below. Try to imagine the previous thoughts of the speakers.

1. _____, how are your children? Are they in school yet?
2. _____, how did it go today? Was the store busy?
3. _____, tell me, how do you like married life?
4. _____, where are you working this week? Every time I see you, you're working for a different company.
5. _____, when did you finally move into your house? You had a lot of trouble finding one, didn't you?

V. BUT and BUT NOT

A. Look at these sentences:

Examples: 1. He is smart. He is lazy. (*but*)
He is smart, but lazy.

2. She is talented. She isn't patient. (*but not*)
She is talented, but not patient.

B. Combine the two sentences with *but* or *but not*. Follow the examples.

1. He has a small apartment. He has a lot of furniture. (*but*)
2. She wants a new job. She can't find one. (*but*)
3. He doesn't study a lot. He always passes his exams. (*but*)
4. He likes tea. He doesn't like coffee. (*but not*)
5. He speaks English. He doesn't speak French. (*but not*)
6. She likes to read magazines. She doesn't like to read books. (*but not*)
7. She can play the piano. She can't play the guitar. (*but not*)
8. I'm working on Friday. I'm not working on Saturday. (*but not*)

UNIT 22
Ali's Future

LESSON 1

361	MR. NIKZAD:	What are we going to do with Ali?
	MRS. NIKZAD:	What do you mean, dear? He's only six.
362/363	MR. NIKZAD:	He'll be seven in a few weeks. It's time to think about his future.
	MRS. NIKZAD:	Oh, dear.
364	MR. NIKZAD:	You spoil him, Zahra.
	MRS. NIKZAD:	And you're too strict. You're always criticizing him.
365	MR. NIKZAD:	Because he never behaves. Why can't Ali be more like Hussein? 365
366	MRS. NIKZAD:	But dear, they are different people. They'll never behave the same way. 366
367	MR. NIKZAD:	We take him to the Fair, and what does he do? 367 He runs away!
	MRS. NIKZAD:	He's a very independent child.
	MR. NIKZAD:	I'll never understand him. And what an imagination! He thinks ice cream vendors are secret agents. He talks to animals and toys.
	MRS. NIKZAD:	All children are like that, dear.
	MR. NIKZAD:	No, Zahra, all children are not like that.
368		You can't make excuses for him forever.

GRAMMATICAL PREVIEW

				Contractions:
Subject Pronouns	Modal: WILL	Verbs		Subject Pronouns + *Will*
I You We They He/She (It)	(+) will (−) won't	go move start take be	to the Fair tomorrow. to New York next year. dinner in half an hour. time off in August. seven years old this Friday.	I'll You'll We'll They'll He'll/ She'll (It'll)

Question: *Will Ali* be seven this year?

Answer: Yes, *he will.*

Question: *Will Ali* be six this year?

Answer: No, *he won't.* He'll be seven.

$$(+) \qquad\qquad (-)$$
Tag Questions: 1. Ali will be seven this year, won't he?
$$(-) \qquad\qquad (+)$$
2. Ali won't be six this year, will he?

Polite Command: Will you please close the door?

Polite Invitation: Won't you please sit down?

SUBSTITUTION DRILLS

1. What are we going to do **with**   Ali?   **Send him to another**
                                                school?
                                   about   Be more strict with him?
                                                Spoil him a little more?

2. It's time to think about his **future.**
                                    education.
                                    grades.
                                    behavior.
                                    career.

3. You **spoil**   him.
           praise
           criticize
           yell at
           punish

4. Why can't Ali **be**   more like Hussein?
                     act
                     talk
                     behave
                     think

5.   **He'll** be seven years old in a few weeks.
       Ali will
       She'll
    Jane will
        I'll

6.
                    We'll go to the Fair tomorrow.
        Hussein and I will
                    You'll
                   They'll
    Mr. and Mrs. Nikzad will

7. What does Ali like? —He likes ice cream.
                                          television.
                                          animals.
                                          mysteries.
                                          secrets.

8. What is Ali like? —He's independent.
                                          creative.
                                          intelligent.
                                          unhappy.
                                          difficult.

9. Who is Ali like? —He's like his cousin.
                                        my friend, John.
                                        the kid downstairs.
                                        all children.

10. You can't make excuses for him forever.
                           apologize
                           cover up
                           lie
                           do his work

CONNECTED DRILL

We take him to the Fair, and what does he do? He runs away.
    give him everything,   leaves home.
    lend him the car,   loses the
                                                              keys.
    buy him new toys,   breaks them.

EXERCISES

1. Complete this dialogue. Use the words below.

are • will • can't • like

MR. NIKZAD: I _____ never understand Ali. What an
                 imagination! He thinks ice cream vendors
                 _____ secret agents. He talks to animals and
                 toys.

MRS. NIKZAD: All children are _____ that, dear.

MR. NIKZAD: No, Zahra, all children _____ not like that.
              You _____ make excuses for him forever.

2. Complete the sentences. Use the words below.

Is • is • Does • like • look

a. What _____ Mr. Nikzad like?
   —He's strict.

b. _____ Ali like Bill O'Neill?
   —Yes, he visits him all the time.

c. What does Ali _____ to eat?
   —Ice cream sandwiches.

d. _____ Hussein more like his father or his mother?
   —He's more like his father.

e. Does Hussein _____ like his mother or his father?
   —His father.

3. Complete the sentences. Use " -'ll " + verb.

Example: How old is he?
　　　　　—He _____ seven in a few weeks. (*be*)
　　　　　He'll be seven in a few weeks.

a. When is she coming?
　　—She _____ here in five minutes. (*be*)

b. I can't take a vacation now. I'm too busy. I _____
　　on vacation in September. (*go*)

c. I have to go. The other phone is ringing. I _____ you
　　later. (*call*)

d. Mary: [*to John*] I had a wonderful summer. I _____
　　never _____ you. (*forget*)

e. The Crawfords are coming for dinner. I want to make
　　something special. Maybe I _____ lamb. (*make*)

f. Can you drive me to the post office?
　　—Sure. I _____ you _____ on my way to work.
　　(*pick up*)

g. You can't go to the party. You have to study.
　　—Don't worry about me. I _____ later tonight. (*study*)

h. Why don't you do your homework now?
　　—I don't want to. I _____ it after dinner. (*do*)

i. Why can't I swim in the lake? The water looks beautiful.
　　—You _____ sorry. The water is very cold. (*be*)

LESSON 2

369 370	MR. NIKZAD:	Last year he misbehaved because he didn't understand English.369 This year you won't be able to use that excuse.370
	MRS. NIKZAD:	Then we'll have to find a school for children like Ali.
371	MR. NIKZAD:	Where will you find a school for stubborn children with bad manners? He won't listen to anybody.371
372	MRS. NIKZAD:	He's not stubborn; he's independent. But don't worry. I'll look for a school for creative children.372
373	MR. NIKZAD:	Won't you ever believe me?373 The boy needs discipline.
	MRS. NIKZAD:	Let me try, Simon. Maybe I can find the right school.
374	MR. NIKZAD:	All right, Zahra. But next year, back in Iran, things will be different.374
375	MRS. NIKZAD:	Be patient, dear. Ali will make you proud one day.375
	MR. NIKZAD:	Where is Ali now?
	MRS. NIKZAD:	Watching T.V.
	MR. NIKZAD:	Are you sure? It's very quiet in there.

SUBSTITUTION DRILLS

1. Last year he misbehaved because he didn't understand English.
it was his first year here.
he was too young.
he missed his friends.
it wasn't the right school for him.

2. This year I won't be able to use that excuse.
take a vacation in September.
live in a big apartment.
go to school in the evening.
pay my taxes on time.

3. He won't listen to anybody.
eat his dinner.
talk to me.
behave.
come to the party.

4. Don't worry. I'll look for a school for children like Ali.
rent a less expensive apartment.
move to a quieter neighborhood.
take a shorter vacation.

5. Won't
   Will   you ever believe me?

6.   I will.
   He won't.
   She
   It
   We
   You
   They

7. Back in Iran,   things will be different.
      home,
      in Europe,
      on the farm,
      at the office,

8. Ali will make you proud one day.
               happy
               sad
               angry

CONNECTED DRILLS

1.   You won't be very late, will you?
  Mr. Nikzad   he?
  Mrs. Nikzad   she?
  The teachers   they?

2. We'll have time to study tonight, won't we?
  I   I?
  You   You?

3. Where will you find a school for Ali?
  When   start to look for a school for him?
  What   tell Ali's teachers?
  How   decide on the right school?

EXERCISES

1. Complete the sentences. Use "won't" + verb.

   a. I have to finish my homework now. I _____ time to do
      it later. (*have*)

   b. The O'Neills are going to a party on Saturday.
      They _____ come to the baseball game. (*be able to*)

   c. Don't be afraid to tell Mr. Nikzad. He _____ at you.
      (*yell*)

d. Mr. Crawford doesn't think Laura is a good secretary.
   He _____ her a good recommendation. (*give*)

e. Ali is too independent. His teachers _____ him. (*like*)

f. What are we going to do about Susan? She _____ her
   dinner. (*eat*)

2. Make questions. Follow the examples.

Example: Ali will go to school in September.
   Will Ali go to school in September?

a. Ali will calm down next year.
b. He won't believe you.
c. She won't do her homework.
d. You'll miss me.
e. Mr. Nikzad will be very angry.
f. They won't speak to each other.

3. Complete the sentences. Use a contraction (subject + -'ll) + verb.

a. Don't worry about Hussein. He _____ his homework.
   (*do*)

b. Can you make something for the party?
   —Sure I _____ an apple pie. (*make*)

c. What can we do for Ted's birthday?
   —I know! We _____ a party! (*have*)

d. They can't find a buyer for the store.
   —Don't worry. I'm sure they _____ it this week. (*sell*)

e. When will you meet me?
   —I _____ for you after the movie. (*wait*)

BONUS DIALOGUE

Ali is watching television in his room.

MRS. NIKZAD:	What are you doing, Ali?
ALI:	Ssh. You have to be very quiet!
MRS. NIKZAD:	Why? What are you doing?
ALI:	Can't you see, Mommy? The *Martians are landing.
MRS. NIKZAD:	Oh. Well, *we're* eating dinner.
ALI:	O.K.
MRS. NIKZAD:	Aren't you coming?
ALI:	No, I'm not.

*Martians - people from the planet Mars.

MRS. NIKZAD: Ali, your father will be very angry.

ALI: No, he won't. He'll be happy.

MRS NIKZAD: Why?

ALI: I ruin his dinner. He always says, "Ali, why do you always ruin my dinner?"

MRS. NIKZAD: He won't say that tonight.

ALI: Then he says, "Why can't you be like Hussein?" I hate Hussein! I don't want to be like him.

MRS. NIKZAD: Ali, that's a terrible thing to say about your brother.

ALI: But it's true.

MRS. NIKZAD: Ali, my little Martian, I won't enjoy my dinner without you. I'll miss you. Won't you come to the table and eat with me?

ALI: O.K. But remember, it's only for you.

MRS. NIKZAD: I'll remember. It'll be our secret.

UNIT 23
Would You Like to Go to the Fair?

LESSON 1

	FRANK YAMAMOTO:	Father?
	MR. YAMAMOTO:	Yes?
376	FRANK:	Wouldn't you like to take a walk to the Fair today?
	MR. YAMAMOTO:	It's Saturday. I have to be in the store.
	FRANK:	I'm sure Jim can take care of the store.
	MR. YAMAMOTO:	I don't like crowds.
377	FRANK:	I know, Father, but it's early. There won't be many people there at this hour. 377
378	MR. YAMAMOTO:	I'd rather go on a weekday. 378 Saturday is our busy day at the store.
379	FRANK:	Take a one-day vacation. 379 I'm sure you'll enjoy it.
	MR. YAMAMOTO:	I don't know, Frank.
380 381	FRANK:	People come from around the world to see the Fair. You're lucky. You live right around the corner. 381

GRAMMATICAL PREVIEW

WOULD

Subject Pronouns	Modal: WOULD	Verbs			Contractions: Subject Pronouns + *would*
I You We They He She (It)	(+) would (−) wouldn't	like to	take go take spend dance	a walk. downtown. a taxi. the day at home. with me.	I'd You'd We'd They'd He'd She'd It'd

Question: *Would* you like to go to the beach today?

Answers: (a) *Yes, I would.*

(b) *No, I wouldn't.* I'd rather spend the day at home.

Tag Questions: 1. You'd like to take a taxi, wouldn't you?

2. You wouldn't like to take a taxi, would you?

SUBSTITUTION DRILLS

1. Would you like to take a walk to the Fair?
go for a walk?
come over for dinner?
go to the party tonight?
spend the day with me?

2.   I'd like to go to the Fair this afternoon.
He'd
She'd
We'd
You'd
They'd

3. What would you like to do today?
—I'd like to take a walk to the Fair.
visit my sister.
go downtown.
go to the beach.
spend the day at home.

4. There won't be many people there at this hour.
this early in the morning.
that late in the afternoon.
until after twelve o'clock.
on a Saturday morning.

5. Take a   one *-day vacation.
three
six
twenty-one
forty-five

---

*Note: *day* is singular. More on this structure in Book 5.

6. People come from **around the world**   **to see the Fair.**
                          all over the world
                          everywhere
                          far and wide
                          the four corners of the earth

7. You live **right around the corner.**
                          only two blocks away.
                          right next door.
                          very close by.
                          so near the Fair.

CONNECTED DRILLS

1.   **What** would you like to **do today?**   —**Go for a swim.**
          Where   go?   —To the beach.
          When   leave?   —At 10 o'clock.
          Who   go out with? —A few friends.
          How   go?   —Let's take a bus.
     How long   stay?   —All day.

2. I'd rather **go to the Fair on a weekday** than **on a weekend.**
                    have a cold drink   hot coffee.
                    take a bus   drive (the car).
                    live in the country   in the city.
                    work late tonight   come in early
                                                             tomorrow.

EXERCISES

1. Choose the right words for the sentences below.

I'd • **I'll** • **Would** • **Do** • **like**

a. _____ you like beer or wine?
   —I'd like a beer, please.

b. _____ you like apples?
   —No, I don't.

c. _____ you type this letter again, please?
   —Certainly. _____ do it right away.

d. Where are you and Frank spending your vacation this year?
   —We're not sure. Frank wants to go to Florida, but _____ rather go to New York.

e. May I take your order?
   —Yes. I'd _____ a hamburger, french fries, and a glass of milk.

2. "Would you like" is a polite way to suggest or offer something. Make polite questions. Follow the example.

Example: (a cup of coffee) —Yes, thank you. I would.
   Would you like a cup of coffee?

a. (a glass of wine)   —No, thank you. I'd like a beer

b. (to spend the day at the beach) —I'm sorry, I can't. I have to work.

c. (to meet me after work tomorrow) —I'd love to, but I have to work late.

d. (half of this orange)   —No, thanks. I'm not hungry

e. (a magazine to read)   —Yes, I would. Thank you.

f. (to take a walk to the park) —Not really. I'm too tired, but thanks for asking me.

3. Make questions with "rather." Follow the example.

Example: (have an apple or an orange)
Would you rather have an apple or an orange?

a. (go out or stay home)
b. (have an ice cream cone or some grapes)
c. (see a western or a war movie)
d. (go with me or with Tom)
e. (buy roses or tulips)

4. Answer the questions. Use "would ('d) like to" and "have/has to."
Follow the example.

Example: Why don't you want to go to the beach? (*stay home*)
I'd like to go to the beach, but I have to stay home.

a. Why don't you want to take a break? (*type this letter*)
b. Why don't you want to go to a movie? (*make dinner*)
c. Why doesn't Miguel want to visit Marta? (*write his mother*)
d. Why doesn't Grandfather want to go the Fair? (*take care of the store*)
e. Why doesn't Michael want to be a painter? (*earn some money*)

LESSON 2

382	MR. YAMAMOTO:	What's the weather like today?
383/384	FRANK:	It's a beautiful spring day. It would be good for you to spend a day in the sun.
385	MR. YAMAMOTO:	Can I get to the Fair by bus?
	FRANK:	It's not far. Take a taxi. It won't be expensive.
	MR. YAMAMOTO:	No. I'll take the bus.
386	FRANK:	O K. Take the number 20. It goes right to the Fair. **386**
387	MR. YAMAMOTO:	Where is my good coat?
388	FRANK:	In the hall closet. But you won't need a coat today. The sun is shining, and it's going to get warm. **388**
389	MR. YAMAMOTO:	Are you sure it's not going to rain?
390	FRANK:	I don't think so, but anything is possible. **390** Your raincoat is in the hall closet, too.
	MR. YAMAMOTO:	You know, Frank, I'm not as young as I was.
	FRANK:	No one is, Father.
	MR. YAMAMOTO:	You're right. Help me with my coat, Frank.
	FRANK:	Have a good time, Father.
	MR. YAMAMOTO:	Thank you, Son.

SUBSTITUTION DRILLS

1. What's the weather like today? —It's hot and humid.
        it like out   cold and damp.
                                         raining.
                                         snowing.
                                         freezing.
                                         nice.
                                         awful.

2.   Spring is my favorite season.
      Summer
   Autumn/Fall
     Winter

3. It's a beautiful spring day.
                      summer evening.
                      fall (autumn) afternoon.
                      winter morning.

4. It's a beautiful day.
       sunny
       rainy
       cloudy
       snowy
       hot and muggy
       wet and humid

5. It's going to get warm.
cool.
cloudy.
foggy.
windy.

6. Are you sure it's not going to rain?
snow?
get cold?
clear up?

7. Anything is possible.
could happen.

8. It would be good for you to spend a day in the sun.
take a vacation.
go to the country.
find a new job.
see your family.

9. Can I get there by bus?
taxi?
subway?
train?
plane?
ship?
boat?

10. The number 20 bus goes right to the Fair.
train station.
airport:
hotel.
center of town.

11. Where is my good   coat?
old
new
tweed
striped

CONNECTED DRILL

Tulips grow **in** spring.
The sun is brightest   summer.
Leaves turn brown   autumn.
Snow falls   winter.

EXERCISES

1. Complete this dialogue. Use the words below.

would • won't • weather • rain • sun • warm

MR. YAMAMOTO: What's the _____ like today?
FRANK: It's a beautiful spring day. It _____ be
good for you to spend a day in the
_____.

MR. YAMAMOTO: Where's my good coat?
FRANK: In the hall closet. But you _____ need a
coat today. It's going to get _____.
MR. YAMAMOTO: Are you sure it's not going to _____?
FRANK: Yes, I'm sure.

2. Make one sentence. Follow the example.

Example: It's a sunny day. It's spring.
It's a sunny spring day.

a.   It's a rainy afternoon. It's autumn.
b.   It's a snowy morning. It's winter.
c.   It's a cold, clear day. It's winter.
d.   It's a cloudy day. It's spring.
e.   It's a hot, muggy day. It's summer.
f.   It's a beautiful evening. It's fall.

3. Answer the questions. Follow the example.

Example: What's the weather like today? (*hot and muggy*)
　　　　　It's hot and muggy.

a. What's the weather like today? (*cold and snowy*)
b. What was the weather like yesterday? (*hot and humid*)
c. What's the weather going to be like tomorrow? (*warm and sunny*)
d. What was the weather like last night? (*damp and foggy*)
e. What's the weather like in fall in New York? (*cool and crisp*)

4. Say the sentences another way. Follow the example.

Example: Let's take a bus to the Fair.
　　　　　Let's go to the Fair by bus.

a. Let's take a taxi to the airport.
b. Let's take the train to the country.
c. Let's take a plane to Paris.
d. Let's take a ship to Hong Kong.
e. Let's take a bus downtown.

5. Say the sentence another way. Follow the example.

   Example: The **sun** is shining today.
   It's a sunny day.

   a. It's **raining** today.
       It's a _____ day.
   b. It's going to **snow** tomorrow.
       It's going to be a _____ day.
   c. There is a lot of **fog** this morning.
       It's a _____ morning.
   d. There are a lot of **clouds** this afternoon.
       It's a _____ afternoon.
   e. The **wind** was strong last night.
       It was a very _____ night.

BONUS DIALOGUE

It's Raining

PEDRO: Excuse me. How much is the bus?

WOMAN: Fifty cents.

PEDRO: Will the driver change a $10 bill?

WOMAN: I don't think so. Oh, here's the bus.
[There is a large splash of water. The bus stops, and the door opens.]

WOMAN: Oh, no!
[Pedro and the woman get on the bus.]

BUS DRIVER: What's the matter, *lady?

WOMAN: Look at me!

BUS DRIVER: You look beautiful to me.

WOMAN: Look at my dress! It's ruined!

BUS DRIVER: I'm sorry, miss.

WOMAN: Is that all you can say? 'I'm sorry, miss.' What about my dress?

PEDRO: What are you going to do about this?

BUS DRIVER: Who are you?

PEDRO: Who do you *think* I am?

BUS DRIVER: Look, mister. I'm sorry. It's raining. The streets are wet.

PEDRO: Let's sit down, dear.

BUS DRIVER: Hey, mister! You forgot to pay!

PEDRO: I did *not* forget. Is the bus company going to pay for a new dress?

BUS DRIVER: Forget it! Forget it! Sit down.

WOMAN: [to Pedro] Very clever. Do you ever pay for the bus?

PEDRO: By the way, my name is . . .

*Lady is not a polite form of address.

UNIT 24

In Mr. Crawford's Office

LESSON 1

	PAULO:	And that, Mr. Crawford, is our plan.
391		We'd like your agency to handle the publicity.
392	MR. CRAWFORD:	Good. Now let me make sure I have all the facts.
	PAULO:	Certainly.
	MR. CRAWFORD:	The Brazilian Pavilion is planning a competition for young artists.
393	PAULO:	Yes, and by the way, the Pavilion will display many of the entries during the final month of the competition.
394	MR. CRAWFORD:	I see. Now, the entries must all be oil paintings, correct? **394**
	PAULO:	Yes.
395	MR. CRAWFORD:	Is there an age limit for the participants?
396/397	PAULO:	We were thinking of thirty or thirty-five. But you must know more about this than I do. You have more experience.
	MR. CRAWFORD:	I think thirty is the right limit. How old are you, Paulo? May I call you Paulo?
	PAULO:	Of course, sir. Twenty-nine.
	MR. CRAWFORD:	You're the same age as my son Michael.
	PAULO:	Yes.
398	MR. CRAWFORD:	Forgive me. Where were we? **398**

SUBSTITUTION DRILLS

1. We'd like your office to **handle the publicity.**
take care of the advertising.
design the brochures.
publish the newsletter.
judge the entries.

2. Now let me make sure **I have all the facts.**
I remember everything.
I didn't forget anything.
we agree on the plan.
we understand each other.

3. We will display many of
the entries during the **final month of the competition.**
last part of the competition.
summer.
month of August.

4. Is there **an age limit for the participants?**
a time limit for the exam?
a deadline for the competition?
a limit to the number of entries?

5.

We You They	were	thinking of thirty or thirty-five.
I	was	
He She		

6. Where were we?
—We were discussing the rules of the competition.
talking about the age limit.
deciding on the number of entries.

7. The entries must   be oil paintings, correct?
have to

8.   Must the entries be oil paintings?
Do the entries have to

9. Must you leave so soon?
make a speech at the meeting?
study tonight?
go to school during the summer?

10. Yes, they must.
we
I
you
he
she

11. Mr. Nikzad is always yelling at his son Ali.
He tells Ali every day. . .

You *mustn't play in the street.
talk to strangers.
bother the ice cream vendor.
pick the flowers in the park.
write on the walls.

*Note: In *mustn't* the first "t" is not pronounced.

CONNECTED DRILLS

1. **You must know more about this than I do.**
    Ali   like ice cream. He eats it every day.
    Suzy   study a lot. She gets good marks in school.
    Paulo   be tired. He worked all day.
    It   be very late. The office is empty.

2. **a.** **Ali isn't eating ice cream.**

    b. I called her six times today, but she was always busy.

    c. Mr. Crawford doesn't need this report today.

    d. Laura and her friends are looking at a map.

He	must not	**be hungry.**
She		want to talk to you.
It		be very important.
They		know their way around the city.

3.

Today is Sunday.	**You**	**don't have to**	**get up early.**
I have a lot of cash.	I		go to the bank.
It's a warm summer day.	You		take a sweater.
Look for another job!	You		work in an office.
It's a holiday today.	We		go to school.

EXERCISES

1. Use the right word(s) to complete the sentences

home • **tired** • **lost** • **cold** • **Paulo** • **in his room**
• **in love**

a. A man and a woman are standing on a street corner. They are looking at map. They look confused. They must be
    _____.

b. It's winter. Marta is going for a walk. She's wearing two sweaters under her coat. It must be very _____ out.

c. Mr. Yamamoto walked around the Fair all day today. He must be _____.

d. It's 6:00. Ali watches television in his room at 6:00. He must be _____.

e. I called the Nikzads a minute ago, but no one answered. They must not be _____.

f. Miguel saw Marta every evening last week. They are always together. They must be _____.

g. Paulo always gives Joana flowers for her birthday. On Joana's birthday, the florist brings a big bouquet of red roses to Joana's apartment. The roses must be from _____.

2. Use ''don't/doesn't have to'' or ''mustn't.''

> **Examples:** 1. It isn't raining.
> *You don't have to take your umbrella.*
>
> 2. There's no parking in front of the hospital entrance.
> *You mustn't park your car there.*

a. Everyone has to be quiet during the exam. You _____ talk to anyone until the exam is over.

b. The Gomezes are moving to San Francisco. Mr. Gomez has a new job, and it starts in September. They _____ move until September.

c. Bill went to the dentist this morning. The dentist found a lot of cavities. He _____ eat so much candy.

d. I'm going to tell you a secret. You _____ tell anyone.

e.   Most department stores have no-smoking signs. You
_____ smoke in these stores.

f.   Thanksgiving is a holiday in the United States. Most people
_____ go to work on Thanksgiving.

g.   The sign above that door says "Exit. Do not enter." You
_____ enter the store that way.

h.   John graduated from college last June and is working now. He
_____ buy textbooks anymore.

i.   Ali asks people questions all the time, and his mother thinks
this is very impolite. She says, "Ali, you _____ ask so
many questions."

j.   There are several restaurants near the office. We _____
eat in the same one every day.

3.   Make a statement about each sentence. Use pronouns and "must."

Example: Miguel's parents and the Monteros come from the same
small town in Colombia. (*know each other*)
They must know each other.

a.   Pedro has many girlfriends. (*like women*)

b.   Jane is sitting in the first row in her English class, and she can't
see the blackboard. (*need glasses*)

c.   My pen won't write. (*be out of ink*)

d.   The Crawfords live in a big expensive house. (*have a lot of
money*)

e.   There is a long line to see the new movie. (*be a good movie*)

LESSON 2

	PAULO:	We were discussing the rules of the competition.
399	MR. CRAWFORD:	Yes. Now, you mentioned a grant. What kind of a grant were you thinking of?399
400	PAULO:	We were going to offer a scholarship, a living allowance, and air fare to and from Brazil. What do you think of that idea?
401 402	MR. CRAWFORD:	Excellent. What about the deadline for the entries.401 Six months from today?402
403 404	PAULO:	Yes. They have to enter by November 1. We'll announce the winner the following month.
405	MR. CRAWFORD:	Good. Well, I can have sample brochures ready for you in a week.
	PAULO:	Fine.
	MR. CRAWFORD:	Then, I'll see you a week from today. Is 2:00 convenient?
	PAULO:	Perfect.

GRAMMATICAL PREVIEW

Past Continuous Tense

Subject Pronouns	BE	Verb + -ing	Time Expression
I He/She/It	(+)was (−)wasn't	talking	about the rules a few minutes ago.
We You They	(+)were (−)weren't		

Affirmative Statement: He *was* talking about the rules.

Negative Statement: He *wasn't* talking about the rules.

Negative Question: *Wasn't* he talking about the rules?

Affirmative Question: *Was* he talking about the rules?

Answers: (a) Yes, he *was*.

(b) No, he *wasn't*.

Tag Questions: 1. He *was* talking about the rules, *wasn't* he?

2. He *wasn't* talking about the rules, *was* he?

Preview Question: *What kind of* course are you taking?

Answer: An English course.

SUBSTITUTION DRILLS

1. What kind of grant were you thinking of?
              scholarship
              course
              school
              trip

2. We were going to offer a scholarship, but we changed our minds.
                enter the competition,
                take a science course,
                attend the opening,
                go to Hong Kong,
                get married in August,

3. What were you doing at 7:00 last night? —I was working.
                                watching T.V.
                                eating dinner.
                                talking to Bill.
                                talking about you

4. We'll announce the winner the following month.
                                    week.
                                    day.
                                    year.

5. I'll have the samples ready in a week.
                            a week to ten days.
                            two weeks.
                            a month.
                            an hour.

6. What about the deadline? Six months from today?
                        Two weeks   yesterday?
                        A month   tomorrow?
                        A week   Sunday?

7. I'll see you again **in a month.**
two weeks from today.
next Thursday at 2:00.
tomorrow.

8. They have to enter **by**   November 1.
no later than
before

CONNECTED DRILLS

1. I wasn't **watching television.** I was **doing my homework.**
picking the flowers.   planting them.
at work on Friday.   washing the car.
sleeping.   resting.
crying.   rubbing my eyes.

2.

I He She	**was**	bothering you this morning,	**wasn't**	**I?** he? she?
We They	were		weren't	we? they?

—Yes, **you were.**
he was.
she was.
you were.
they were.

3.

You	weren't	sleeping during the speeches,	were	you?
They				they?
He She	wasn't		was	he? she?

—No, **I wasn't.**
　　　they weren't.
　　　he wasn't.
　　　she wasn't.

4. What kind of
　　scholarship are they offering?　　—**A full tuition scholarship.**
　　building is it?　　　　　　　　　　—A modern glass building.
　　school was it?　　　　　　　　　　—A girls' school.
　　ice cream do you like best?　　　　—Vanilla.
　　car did she buy?　　　　　　　　　—A sports car.
　　music do you like?　　　　　　　　—Classical and rock music.

EXERCISES

1. Here is Paulo's schedule for yesterday:

MONDAY

● 7:00	ate breakfast
9:30	talked to Mr. Crawford
12:00	ate lunch
1:00	planned the exhibition
2:30	took a break
5:30	had a drink with Bill
6:30	wrote my speech
● 8:00	ate dinner
9:00	watched T.V.
11:00	went to sleep

Answer these questions. Follow the example.

What was Paulo doing at 7:05? *He was eating breakfast.*

         9:35?
        12:05?
         1:05?
         2:35?
         5:35?
         6:35?
         8:05?
         9:05?
       11:30?

2. Make tag questions.

Examples: 1. His office was handling the publicity.
            His office was handling the publicity, wasn't it?

          2. You weren't sleeping.
            You weren't sleeping, were you?

a. Ali wasn't watching television.
b. They were washing the car.

c. Laura wasn't attending college last year.
d. The diplomats weren't making speeches.
e. The girls were working at a flower shop after school.

3. Make questions with "What kind of."

Example: I went to a boys' **school.**
What kind of school did you go to?

.a. We were listening to classical **music.**
b. Michael was asking about a full-tuition **scholarship.**
c. I'm going to buy a sports **car.**
d. He's an eye **doctor.**
e. She wants to buy a fancy **dress.**
f. They bought a big old **house.**

BONUS DIALOGUE

MR. CRAWFORD: [*walking to the door with Paulo*] Ms. Segura, Mr. Farias is leaving now. Good-bye, Paulo.

PAULO: Good-bye, Mr. Crawford. And we'll see you and Mrs. Crawford for dinner on Wednesday.

MR. CRAWFORD: We're looking forward to it. [*They shake hands and Paulo leaves. Mr. Crawford returns to his desk. Laura enters.*]

MR. CRAWFORD: Were there any calls?

LAURA: Yes. Your wife called fifteen minutes ago.

MR. CRAWFORD: Did she leave a message?

LAURA: No, sir. And your next appointment is here. Mr. Robert Gardner.

MR. CRAWFORD: Send him in, please.

LAURA: Yes, sir.

UNIT 25
Claire's First Day

LESSON 1

	LAURA:	Your coat, Mr. Farias.
	PAULO:	Thank you, Ms. Segura. Good day.
406	LAURA:	Good day, sir. [to Claire, the new secretary] As you see, Claire, the office is very formal.406
407	CLAIRE:	Yes, I realized that when Mr. Crawford interviewed me.
408	LAURA:	Well, let's go on. The files are easy. We keep our files in alphabetical order.408
	CLAIRE:	Who handles the accounts?
409	LAURA:	We have an accountant. He comes in once a month and *goes over the books.409
	CLAIRE:	Laura, may I ask you a question?
	LAURA:	Of course.
410	CLAIRE:	May I ask why you're leaving?
411	LAURA:	I'd rather not say.
	CLAIRE:	I understand. I'm sorry.
412	LAURA:	No, don't apologize. Where were we? Oh, yes. Well, we keep the office supplies in this cabinet—paper, typewriter ribbons, pads, pencils, pens, envelopes, etc.412

*goes over the books - examines the accounts

GRAMMATICAL PREVIEW

Review *Wh-* Questions

a. with *BE*

Why	is Laura	leaving?
Who	is	at the door?

b. With *MODALS*

What	would you	like for dinner?
Who	will	win?

c. With auxiliary *DO*

How long	did Laura	work there?
Who	did you	speak to at the office?

Embedded *Wh-* Clauses

*I don't know	why	Laura is	leaving
**Do you know	who	is	at the door
	what	you would	like for dinner
	who	will	win
	how long	Laura worked	there
	who	you spoke to	at the office

*Sentences end with a period.
**Sentences end with a question mark.

SUBSTITUTION DRILLS

1. May I ask you why   you're leaving?
                    when
                    what time

2. **I don't know** why Laura quit.
    I'm not sure
    I wonder
    I can't say
    I'd like to know
    I have no idea

3. Claire doesn't know why Laura quit.
                      what Mr. Crawford is like.
                      when she will go home tonight.
                      where the newsletter file is.
                      how Mr. Crawford treats his employees.
                      how long Laura worked for the firm.
                      how much she can learn the first day.
                      how many people work for Mr. Crawford.

4.   **Do you know** why Laura quit?
    Can you tell me
    May I ask you
    Do you remember
    Did anyone ask
    Can you explain

5. As you see,   the office is very formal.
            will notice,
            know,
            can imagine,
            mentioned,

6. I realized that when he **interviewed me.**
   asked me for three references.
   gave me his business card.
   opened the door for me.
   shook my hand.

7. I found that out **when** I accepted the job.
   before
   after

8. Let's **go on.**
   continue.

9. The accountant
   comes in **once a month** and goes over the books.
   twice a year
   three times a week
   every now and then
   from time to time

10. We keep the **supplies—pens, paper,** etc., in this cabinet.
   magazines—sports, news,
   snacks—cookies, fruit,
   forms—insurance, personnel,

EXERCISES

1. Make one question. Follow the examples.

Examples: 1. Why did Laura resign? Do you know?
Do you know why Laura resigned?

2. When did she take the job? Can you tell me?
Can you tell me when she took the job?

a. Where did everybody go? Do you know?
b. How did Mr. Crawford treat Laura? Can you tell me?
c. When did they get divorced? Do you remember?
d. What kind of job did she apply for? Do you know?
e. What did he say? Can you remember?
f. Why did Mr. Crawford hire a new secretary? Don't you know?
g. Where did you buy your sweater? May I ask you?

2. Make one statement. Follow the example.

Example: What is he laughing at? I don't know.
I don't know what he's laughing at.

a. What does this word mean? I don't know.
b. Which course are you going to take? I'd like to know.
c. When did it start to rain? I didn't notice.
d. Where will Laura find another job? I don't know.
e. Why did Laura quit? No one knows.

3. Make one statement. Follow the example.

Example: Whose book is this? Nobody knows.
Nobody knows whose book this is.

a. Whose car is this? I don't know.
b. How much is the air fare to Brazil? I'm not sure.
c. Where was she? We don't know.
d. What time is it? I don't know.
e. What country is she from? I can't remember.
f. How late is the store open? I don't know.

4. Make one question. Follow the example.

Example: Who is applying for the job? Do you know?
Do you know who is applying for the job?

a. How many people were at the opening? Can you remember?
b. Who pays the bills? Can anybody tell me?
c. Who wrote the article? Do you know?
d. What happened? Did you hear?
e. Who is taking care of the children tonight? Do you know?

5. Make two sentences, one with "before" and one with "after."

Example: I cleaned the house at 5:00. The guests arrived at 7:00.
    Student 1: *I cleaned the house before the guests arrived.*
    Student 2: *The guests arrived after I cleaned the house.*

a. We saw a movie at 7:00. We ate dinner at 9:00.
b. We called John's house at 9:00. You left his house at 8:00.
c. Miguel went to sleep at 10:00. Paulo went out at 11:00.
d. I took Suzy to the park at 2:00. We ate lunch at 1:00.

6. Complete the sentences. Use "when."

Example: I was not home at 7:00. You called at 7:00.
I was not home when you called.

a. I left the house at 9:00. Laura arrived at 9:00.
I left the house _____.

b. I thought about you this afternoon. I saw your sister this
afternoon.
I thought about you _____.

c. I went to sleep at 12:00. The movie ended at 12:00.
I went to sleep _____.

d. I woke up at 8:00. The alarm went off at 8:00.
I woke up _____.

LESSON 2

413 LAURA: Do you have any questions so far?

414 CLAIRE: Yes. How often do you work late?

415 LAURA: Hardly ever.₄₁₅ Mr. Crawford doesn't like to pay overtime.

416 CLAIRE: Good. Because I don't know if I can stay late. ₄₁₆ I go to school at night.

LAURA: What are you studying?

417 CLAIRE: Law. When I was a girl, I wanted to be a lawyer.₄₁₇ And I'm going to be one.

418 LAURA: I admire you. It must be difficult to work while you're going to school. ₄₁₈

CLAIRE: It is, but it's what I want to do.

LAURA: Good luck. Oh, I almost forgot. We publish a World's

419 Fair newsletter. Henry Leeds is the editor. His office is across the hall. ₄₁₉ I think that's it.

CLAIRE: Uh—where's the ladies' room?

LAURA: Oh, around the corner, second door on the left.

CLAIRE: I want to thank you for all your help.

LAURA: I was happy to do it. Here are the keys. After 5:00

420 today, it's all yours. One more thing, be on time! He gets angry when you're late.₄₂₀

GRAMMATICAL PREVIEW

When and *while* sometimes have the same meaning, "at that time."
While usually indicates duration.

1. PRESENT → PRESENT or PRESENT CONTINUOUS.

    a. It is difficult to work **while** you're going to school.
    when

    b. My boss gets angry **when** I'm late.

2. PAST CONTINUOUS (or PAST) → PAST CONTINUOUS (or PAST)

a. Laura was typing   **while** Mr. Crawford was interviewing Claire.
   Laura left the office **when** Mr. Crawford was interviewing Claire.
   Laura typed a letter   Mr. Crawford interviewed Claire.

b. * I woke up   **when** my alarm clock rang.
   I took notes   the teacher spoke.

3. FUTURE → PRESENT

    Claire's going to answer the phone **when** Laura's out to lunch.
    while

Note: We can also place the time clauses at the beginning of the
        sentence. We must use a comma.
        a. **When** my alarm clock rang, I woke up.
        b. **While** you were sleeping, I was making dinner.

Preview Question: *How often* do you work late?

Answer: Once or twice a week.

* *Note:* This is a cause and effect.

SUBSTITUTION DRILLS

1. It must be difficult to work while **you are going to school.**
you are studying for exams.
the baby is crying.
the television is on.

2. Laura **talked to Claire**   while Mr. Crawford met with Paulo.
called a client
went out to lunch
spoke to Mrs. Crawford
typed a letter

3. While Mr. Crawford was
interviewing Claire,   Laura was looking for a new job.
speaking to Paulo,
eating lunch,
finding errors,
complaining to his wife,

4. He gets angry when you're late.
you take long lunches.
he finds mistakes.
I leave early.
we miss a deadline.

5. When I was a girl, I wanted to be a lawyer.
lived in Paris.
took dancing lessons.
hated boys.

6. Do you have any questions so far?
up to now?
at this point?

7. How often do you work late? —Hardly ever.
—Rarely.
—Not very often.
—Every day.
—Once or twice a week.
—Three or four times a semester.

8. How often do you work late?
take a taxi to work?
go to the dentist?
call your family?
cook dinner?

9. I don't know if I can stay late.
whether I'll be able to study.
Laura really wants to be a secretary.
Claire is going to stay.

CONNECTED DRILLS

1. Where's the **ladies' room?—Around the corner, second door on the left.**

men's room?—Down the hall, third door on the right.

accounting office?—Across the hall from the water fountain.

English Department?—On the fifth floor. Across from the elevator.

mailbox?—Turn right at the corner. Then walk straight ahead, about a block.

2. **Can Claire work late?**
Will she be home tonight?
Is it raining? ..
Did Mr. Crawford go out to lunch?
Does it take long to get to the airport?

—I don't know if **Claire can work late.**
she'll be home tonight.
it's raining.
Mr. Crawford went out to lunch.
it takes long to get to the airport.

EXERCISES

1. Make questions with "How often" and answer them.

Example: Laura **hardly ever** works late.
Student 1: *How often does she work late?*
Student 2: *Hardly ever.*

a. The accountant comes in **once a month.**
b. The firm publishes a newsletter **twice a month.**
c. Mrs. Crawford's sister is **hardly ever** in New York.
d. It snows in Montreal **ten or twenty times a winter**
e. Laura **rarely** works overtime.
f. Mr. Crawford **never** praises his employees.
g. I go to the dentist **once a year.**

2. Combine the sentences with "while" and "when."

Example: I was studying. Marta was talking on the phone.
1. *I was studying while Marta was talking on the phone.*
2. *I was studying when Marta was talking on the phone.*

a. Claire's going to answer the phone. Laura's out to lunch.
b. I'm going to take care of the store. Jack's on vacation.
c. Miguel stayed home. Pedro went to the movies.
d. I was typing my report. Nora was cooking dinner.
e. Peggy helped her mother. Suzy was dressing for a party.

3. Combine the sentences with "when." Follow the example.

Example: The phone rang. I woke up.
I woke up when the phone rang.

a. Paulo walked in. I hung up the phone.
b. The movie ended. I cried.
c. The guests arrived. I turned off the television.
d. It started to snow. I went home.
e. It started to rain. I opened my umbrella.

4   Make two questions with "if" and "whether." Follow the example.

Example: Does Bill like his job? Do you know?
   1. *Do you know if Bill likes his job?*
   2. *Do you know whether Bill likes his job?*

a.   Are the Nikzads going back to Iran next year? Do you know?
b.   Is there a men's room on this floor? Can you tell me?
c.   Did anyone call while I was out? Can you tell me?
d.   Do you have to fill out an application before the interview? Do
      you know?
e.   Did Mr. Crawford say anything about vacations? Do you
      remember?
f.   Does this bus go to the Fair? Do you know?

5.   Make two statements with "if" and "whether." Follow the
   example.

Example: Can we go to the beach this weekend? I don't know.
   1. *I don't know if we can go to the beach this
      weekend.*
   2. *I don't know whether we can go to the beach this
      weekend.*

a.   Will Michael come to the party? I don't know.
b.   Did they enjoy their vacation? I wonder.
c.   Will you remember me when you're back home? I wonder.
d.   Can Claire get a raise after six months? I'm not sure.
e.   Do we have to stand in line all day? I wonder.
f.   Are there any apartments near the university? I'd like to know.
g.   Were they talking about me? I wonder.

6. Someone is asking you for directions. Match the questions with the answers.

Questions	*Answers*
a: Where's the ladies' room?	Second door on the left.
b. Where's the men's room?	Walk straight ahead, turn right.
c. Where's Mr. Crawford's office?	Third door on the left.
d. Where's the newsletter office?	First door on the left.
e. Where's the elevator?	At the other end of the hall.
f. Where's the water fountain?	Next to the elevator.
g. Where's the mailbox?	First door on the right.

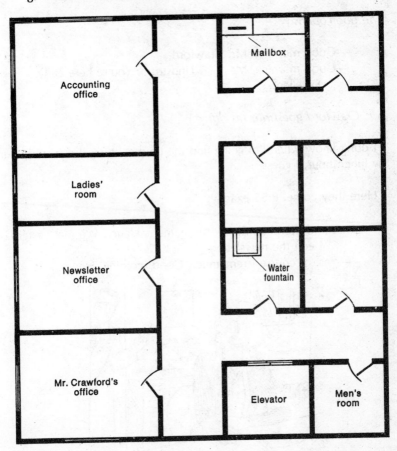

You are —— X
here

BONUS READING

[It's Claire's first day without Laura.]

What am I doing here? What's wrong with this office? Everyone's so quiet. Nobody talks, nobody smiles. Oh well, yesterday was only the first day, and things can change. In any case, it won't last forever.

All right. It's 8:30. Where is everybody? You're early, Claire. Relax. Look around. I wonder where the newsletter file is.

[*The door opens.*]

    —Good morning, Mr. Crawford.
    —Good morning, Ms. . . . Lindstrom. You're here early.
      Excellent.

[*Mr. Crawford goes into his office.*]

I don't know when I'm going find the time to study. I can study during ny lunch hour, I guess.

Here they come. 8:55 exactly.

    —Good morning, Claire. My name is Henry. We met yesterday.
      I edit the newsletter.
    —Yes, of course I remember. Good morning, Henry.

UNIT 26
Reading and Refocus
LESSON 1

A Letter from Miguel's Mother

Dear Miguel,

421 Who is this girl, Marta, in the photograph? She is very pretty. Oh, my poor Miguel! I know you are lonely, but you are so young! Don't ruin your life. You have to continue your studies or you'll never find a good job.**421** I'm glad you are
422 having a good time, but we worry about you. We don't even
423 know who she is.**422** Is she a nice girl? Is she from a good
424 family?**423** Can you tell me what her father does?**424** You
425 won't do anything foolish, will you, Miguel? You don't know how important you are to us.**425**

426 Do you remember the Monteros? They moved to New York about seven years ago. They have a daughter, a very
427/428 pretty girl.**426** She's just about your age.**427** They won't recognize you, of course, but they'll remember us, and they'll be very happy to see you.**428** The girl's name is Maria. I'm sure you'll find the number in the telephone book. His first name is Fernando.

429 Forgive me, Miguel. I know you are a man now, but you are also my son. I worry about you, and I suppose I always will.**429**

Love,

Mama

430 P.S. Write soon.

Questions about "A Letter from Miguel's Mother"

Fact:
The answers are *clear* in the story.

1. Is there only one person or are there at least two people in the photograph?
2. What does Miguel's mother want to know about Marta?
3. Does Miguel's mother think he is having a good time?
4. Do the Monteros have a son or a daughter?
5. Will the Monteros recognize Miguel?
6. Where can Miguel find the Monteros' telephone number?

Inference:
You can *guess the right answers* from the story.

1. Does Mrs. Morales miss Miguel?
2. Why is Miguel's mother asking him so many questions about Marta?
3. Do you think Miguel tells his mother about many girls, or is there something special about Marta?
4. Does Michael look the same as he did seven years ago, or does he look different?
5. Why does Miguel's mother want her son to call the Monteros?
6. Is there more than one Montero in the telephone book?

To the Student:
There are *no wrong answers* to these questions.

1. Do you think Miguel will or won't call the Monteros?
2. Do you think Miguel's mother really thinks her son is a man?
3. What do you think Miguel's parents' hopes are?
4. Do you live near or far from your parents?
5. Do your parents often write to you?
6. Do you like to write letters?

USING YOUR ENGLISH

I. The PRESENT TENSE and the "WILL" Future —

A. **Examples:** 1. Ali loves ice cream.
Ali will always love ice cream.
Ali loves ice cream, and he always will.

2. Paulo is very serious.
Paulo will always be very serious.
Paulo is very serious, and he always will be.

B. Combine the sentences with *and*.

1. My mother doesn't like to travel. My mother will never like to travel.
2. Pedro loves beautiful women. Pedro will always love beautiful women.
3. Baseball is exciting. Baseball will always be exciting.
4. In July it is hot in Washington. In July it will always be hot in Washington
5. Mr. Tweed doesn't like children. Mr. Tweed will never like children.

II. TALKING ABOUT THE FUTURE

A. To discuss the future, we can use:

1. PRESENT CONTINUOUS: a. We're *eating* dinner at 7:00.
b. We're *leaving* tomorrow.

We sometimes use the present continuous tense to discuss a future event which is the result of a plan.

2. SIMPLE PRESENT: a. Dinner *is* at 7:00.
b. We *leave* tomorrow.

We sometimes use the simple present tense to discuss a future event based on a schedule or timetable.

3. "GOING TO": a. We're going to *eat* dinner at 7:00.
b. We're going to *leave* tomorrow.

4. "WILL": a. We'll *eat* dinner at 7:00.
b. We'll *leave* tomorrow.

B. Here are some common uses of *going to* and *will* to talk about the future.

1. "WILL"

a. To predict future events:
   1) It *will rain* tomorrow.
   2) In the year 2050, everyone *will own* a computer.

b. In formal speech:
   1) The President *will* now *speak* to the nation.
   2) The Queen *will* now *open* Parliament.

c. To refuse to do something:
   1) Ali *won't eat* his dinner.
   2) I *won't grow up*.

d. To make promises:
   1) I'll *love* you forever!
   2) I'll *help* you with your homework.

2. "GOING TO"

a. To discuss plans:
   1) I'm *going to* take a vacation next summer.
   2) I'm *going to* have a party.

b. To discuss events based on present causes:
   1) It's *going to* rain soon.
   2) I'm *going to* cry.

C. Use *will* or *going to* in the dialogue below. Sometimes one is preferable, but sometimes both are correct.

MAN 1:   There's a bug in my salad!

MAN 2:   I _____ call the waiter. Excuse me. _____ you come over here please?

WAITER: Yes?

MAN 1:   There's a bug in my salad. And by the way, the rolls are stale.

WAITER: Hmmmmmmmmmmmn. Uh. . .

MAN 2:   Well? _____ you _____ just stand there?

WAITER: I don't see anything in the salad.

MAN 2:   Look, I _____ call the manager.

MAN 1:   My wife _____ be here in a few minutes.
          She _____ eat a thing when she hears about this

WAITER: Very well. I _____ bring you another salad.

MAN 2:   And what about the rolls?

WAITER: I _____ be right back.

MAN 1:   I didn't like him at all.

MAN 2:   I didn't either. I _____ write a letter to the owner.

III. EMBEDDED QUESTIONS

A. Sometimes we ask two questions in one sentence. When we do this, we are usually trying to be polite.

Example: *Can you tell me what her father does?*
    (*Question 1:* What does her father do?
    Polite Question: Can you tell me?)

B. Make two new questions.
    Use *Do you know?* and *Can you tell me?*

Examples: 1. Where is the newsletter file?
        a. *Do you know where the newsletter file is?*
        b. *Can you tell me where the newsletter file is?*

    2. What does her father do?
        a. *Do you know what her father does?*
        b. *Can you tell me what her father does?*

1. What is Mr. Crawford like?
2. Where is Miguel's mother?
3. When is Miguel going home?
4. What kind of car does he drive?
5. When does the bus come?
6. Why did they leave the country?
7. What does he do?
8. Where did they go?
9. What bus do I take?
10. How many children do they have?

1v. PLACE AND TIME

A. We usually talk about place before time when we have both at the end of the sentence.

	PLACE	TIME

Example: They moved to New York about seven years ago.

B. Choose a place and time and make seven sentences.

		PLACE	TIME
1.	He lived	at his house	in the summer.
2.	We always take a walk	to the country	tonight.
3.	I don't like to work	at the movies	on the weekend.
4.	We go	in the sun	before dinner.
5.	We're going to have a good time	on the beach	at noon.
6.	We are eating lunch	in England	at 9:30.
7.	Meet me	at the station	during the war.

Example: He lived *in England during the war.*

LESSON 2

A Day at the Fair

431/432   It was a warm day, warm for April.₄₃₁ People were
walking around the Fair with their coats over their arms.₄₃₂

433   The sun was bright, and there were little white clouds in the
blue sky.₄₃₃ The trees wore a light green smile.

At noon the Saturday crowd was very large. Adults were
laughing, children were crying, and everyone was having a

434   good time. A thousand vendors were selling ice cream, hot
435   dogs, and cold drinks.₄₃₄ It was a beautiful, spring morning—
the kind you want to last forever.₄₃₅

436   Later in the afternoon, the sun was not so bright, the sky
437   not so blue.₄₃₆ The little white clouds were now large and
438   gray.₄₃₇ There was a drop here, a drop there . . . then ten
439   thousand noisy drops.₄₃₈ People shouted and ran in every
440   direction.₄₃₉ Then there was silence, the sun, the blue sky,
and a rainbow.₄₄₀

Questions about "A Day at the Fair"

Fact:
The answers are *clear* in the story.

1. Was it a warm spring day?
2. Were there many people at the Fair that day or only a few?
3. Was anyone having a bad time?
4. Who was selling ice cream, hot dogs, and cold drinks?
5. Did it rain in the early or the late afternoon?
6. What followed the rain?

Inference:
You can *guess the right answer* from the story.

1. Was the weather more like summer or winter that morning?
2. Why did people bring their coats with them?
3. Is the Fair usually busy on Saturdays?
4. Was business good for the vendors?
5. How did the people at the Fair know it was going to rain?
6. Was the rain heavy or light?

To the Student:
There are *no wrong answers* to these questions.

1. Is April a spring or fall month in your country?
2. How does spring make you feel?
3. Does it often rain in your country in April?
4. Do you like to walk in the rain?
5. Do people spend more time outside or inside in your country?
6. What does "The trees wore a light green smile" mean to you?

USING YOUR ENGLISH

I. NOT SO

A. *Not so* can mean "not as (*adjective*) as."
In the reading, *The sky was not so blue.* = "It was not as blue
as it was before."

B. Here are some common English comparisons. Disagree with the
opinions using *not so.*

Example: The baby was **as good as gold** last night.
Oh, come on. She *wasn't so good!* She cried for an
hour!

1. That dog is **as ugly as sin.**
   —Listen, don't talk like that. It's not kind. In any case, the dog
   _____.

2. My father doesn't understand me. He's **as old as the hills,** and
   his ideas are, too.
   —Oh, come on! He's really _____. He just seems that
   way to you because you're so young.

3. Mary's just **as sweet as pie.** I like her a lot.
   —She must like you. She's _____ to other people.

4. John's **as smart as a whip.** He graduated number one from his
   school.
   —Oh, he's _____. He just studies a lot.

5. My granddaughter is **as cute as a button.**
   —She's _____. My grandson is cuter.

6. You look **as fresh as a *daisy.**
   —I'm glad I look it, because I do _____ feel
   _____! I had only three hours' sleep last night.

* **a daisy** is a flower.

II. WHAT KIND(S) OF

A. 1. We use the general question, "What kind of . . . ?" when
we want somebody to:

Name
Describe } something.
Explain

For example: *What kind(s) of car(s) do you like?*

Names: a Toyota, a Ford, Volkswagens, Cadillacs, etc.
Descriptions: old, modern, expensive, American comfortable,
etc.
Explanations: for driving in the city, for racing, for taking trips,
etc.

2. We can ask about one car or many cars.

Examples: a. What *kind* of car . . . ?/ What *kind* of *fruit* . . . ?
We expect *one* name, description, or explanation.

b. What *kind*
         kinds } of cars . . . ?/What *kinds* of *fruit* . . . ?

We expect *more than one* name, description, or
explanation.

B. Make questions with *What kind* or *What kinds*.

Examples: 1. I bought **a Toyota.**
What kind of car did you buy?

2. I like **Volkswagens and Fords.**
What kinds of cars do you like?

1. He has a **green** car.
2. She drives a **sports** car.
3. They make **Japanese, American,** and **European** cars in the United States.
4. I like **old** cars.
5. The store sells **fresh** fruit.
6. They sell **apples, peaches, pears, melons, and oranges.**
7. It's a **fruit** knife.
8. This knife is **for cutting fruit.**
9. We sell **vanilla and chocolate** ice cream.
10. I like to read **detective and adventure** stories.
11. We have four *pets—**two cats and two dogs.**

III. ARTICLES: *A, AN, THE*

A. 1. The first time we mention an unidentified thing (singular), we use *a* or *an*. After that, we use *the*.

Unidentified	**Identified**
We saw *an* elephant, *a* bear, and *a* giraffe at the zoo.	*The* elephant and *the* giraffe were very tall, but *the* bear wasn't.

2. When we speak of a non-limited thing (plural or mass noun) we usually use *no article*. However, when we limit the thing, we use *the*.

Non-Limited	**Limited**
Milk is healthy.	*The* milk from the farm is always fresh.
Music is relaxing.	*The* music in that play was wonderful.
Dogs are friendly animals.	*The* dogs in my neighborhood make too much noise.

* *Pets* are animals people keep for companionship.

3. Sometimes we use *the* before a noun the first time we mention it. This happens when the thing is familiar, or when the identity is obvious.

> *The* sun is bright today.
> Close *the* door.
> Put your clothes in *the* closet.
> *The* children are at school.

B. Use *a, an, the,* or *X* if no article is necessary

1. I'm going to get _____ cup of coffee.
2. _____ Coffee is getting very expensive these days.
3. Everyone in _____ class likes _____ teacher.
4. _____ Life seems very short sometimes.
5. _____ moon is full tonight.

6. I'm not hungry. I had _____ apple a few minutes ago.
7. _____ house next to ours is a hundred years old.
8. English is not _____ easy language.
9. _____ capital of the United States is Washington, D.C.
10. I bought _____ bottle of milk this morning.

IV. TO LAST

A. When we say something *lasts,* we are talking about an amount of time.

Examples: 1. The movie *lasts* two hours. (It begins at 6:30 and ends at 8:30.)

2. Their marriage *lasted* ten years. (They got married in 1965 and got divorced in 1975.)

3. The fruit *won't last* a week. (*Either*: There is not enough, people will eat it all before the week is over, *or* it will spoil before the week is over.

B. Use *lasts, lasted,* or *won't last* to fill in the blanks.

1. I'm not going to class tonight. It_____two hours, and I'm very tired.
2. I was at a meeting from 4:00 to 6:00. That wasn't too long. The meeting only _____ two hours.
3. World War II began in 1939 and ended in 1945. It _____ six years.
4. I just bought a quart of milk. That's not enough. It _____ more than a day.
5. They hired Al in June and fired him in September. He _____ only three months.
6. We started dinner at 8:00 and finished at midnight. Dinner _____ four hours.

LESSON 3

Laura Wonders

441   I admire Claire. She works all day and goes to school at night. She knows where she's going and what she wants, and she's willing to work for it.₄₄₁

442   Am I? In my first job, I was a secretary. When I married
443   my husband, I quit.₄₄₂ After I left him, I went back to the same office.₄₄₃ I never thought about other possibilities.
444   When I came here, I got a job right away.₄₄₄ I was happy
445   with anything.₄₄₅ Now I'd like a change.
446   First things first.₄₄₆ What skills do I have?
       —O.K. I can do anything.
       —Anything?
       —Yes, anything.
       —Come on now, Laura. Be realistic.
       —All right, almost anything. I can speak, read, and write
447   English and Spanish. I can run an office.₄₄₇ I'm friendly
448   and competent. Uh . . . there must be more.₄₄₈ Oh, yes, I type and take shorthand in two languages.

449   —Well, then, if you can do all that, you don't have to work for the Mr. Crawfords of the world!₄₄₉
       —But, what will I do, then?
450   —Well, what kind of job would you like?₄₅₀ Do you want to work in an office again? There's *so much* to think about.

Questions about "Laura Wonders"

Fact:
The answers are *clear* in the story.

1. Does Laura respect Claire?
2. What kind of work was Laura doing when she married her husband?
3. Did Laura go back to work when she left her husband, or did she remarry?
4. Did she look for a job for a long time when she arrived in New York?
5. What languages can Laura speak?
6. Is Laura going to think about the kind of job she would like, or is she going to take anything?

Inference:
You can *guess the right answers* from the story.

1. Does Laura believe success comes from hard work, or does she believe some people are luckier than others?
2. Did Laura work while she was married?
3. Does Laura want to be a secretary again, or does she want a big change?
4. Does Laura think she has any choices now?
5. Why does Laura want a change now?
6. Why does Laura say, "Be realistic"?

To the Student:
There are *no wrong answers* to these questions.

1. Do you think Laura will get married again?
2. What kind of job would Laura like?
3. Do you think it's exciting to look for a new job?
4. Would you rather work or stay home all day?
5. Is it easier for a man or a woman to find a job?
6. What skills do you need to do your job?

USING YOUR ENGLISH

I. TO BE WILLING TO

A. 1. *To be willing to do something* means that someone is ready to do it, even when the situation is not pleasant. Don't confuse it with the modal *will* which usually shows future time.

Examples: a. *I'm willing to* study because I want to learn.
b. I don't agree, but *I'm willing to* listen to you.

2. *Not willing to do something* shows that someone doesn't want to do something, or refuses, like "won't." Again, don't confuse it with future time.

Examples: a. Laura *is not willing to* work for someone like Mr. Crawford again.
b. The doctor *is not willing to* give out information about his patients.

B. Complete the sentences with the correct form of *to be willing to.*

1. She doesn't speak English very well, but she _____ learn.
2. I _____ not _____ answer all the questions on this application.
3. Her parents _____ pay for her college education.
4. Our teacher is very patient. He _____ always _____ answer our questions.
5. _____ you _____ work overtime?
6. I _____ lend you the money, but I don't like the idea.
7. _____ Michael _____ give up art?
8. The Brazilian Pavilion _____ pay the contest winner's air fare to Brazil.
9. I don't like to cook, but I _____ make dinner tonight.
10. We _____ hear everyone's opinion before we make a decision.

II. WOULD LIKE and LIKE

A. *Would like* is a polite way to say "want."

Examples:
1. *I'd like a cup of coffee.*
2. *I would like to go home now.*
3. *Would you like to have dinner with us tonight?*

B. Fill in the sentences below with the correct form of *like* (affirmative or negative) or *would like*.

1. A: _____ you _____ to go out for a pizza?
   B: No, thanks. I don't have the time. Anyway, I _____ really _____ pizza. (*neg.*) It's too spicy.

2. A: _____ you _____ westerns?
   B: What's a western?
   A: A cowboy movie. There's one playing down the street. _____ you _____ to see it?

3. VENDOR: May I help you?
   CUSTOMER: Uh. . .
   VENDOR: What _____ you _____ ?
   CUSTOMER: I _____ a strawberry ice cream cone.
   VENDOR: Sorry, I don't have strawberry. _____ you _____ a vanilla cone?
   CUSTOMER: No, thanks. I _____ _____ vanilla. (*neg.*)

4. A: What are you going to be when you grow up?
   B: I _____ to be an airline pilot.
   A: An airline pilot?? But you _____ _____ to fly. (*neg.*) You're scared of airplanes.
   B: You're right. But I _____ to dream.

III. THE PAST CONTINUOUS TENSE

A. We use the past continuous tense to talk about a past event that had some duration.

1. Sometimes it shows two actions which were going on at the same time.

Example: *I was working in the garden while the children were watching T.V.*

2. Sometimes it focuses on one action which was going on when another event happened.

Examples: a. *I was crossing the street when I saw the accident.*
b. *Who were you talking to?* (when I saw you)
c. *The last time I saw Laura, she was working for Mr. Crawford.* (Maybe Laura is working for him now. We don't know.)

B. Use *the past* or *the past continuous* form of the verbs in parentheses.

WOMAN: Officer, I _____ my wedding ring. (*lose*)
POLICEMAN: When _____ you _____ it was gone? (*notice*)
WOMAN: I _____ my hands when I _____ it wasn't on my finger. (*wash/realize*)
POLICEMAN: Was anyone with you when you _____ it was gone? (*discover*)
WOMAN: Yes. My daughter, Alice.
POLICEMAN· Where is she now?
WOMAN: I don't know. The last time I _____ her, she _____ for it. Oh, here she is. (*see/look*)
ALICE: Mother, I . . .
WOMAN: Alice, I _____ just _____ this officer about my ring. (*tell*)
ALICE: Well, I _____ it a few minutes ago. (*find*)
WOMAN: Where _____ you _____ it? (*find*)
ALICE: Inside a piece of cake.
WOMAN: What??
ALICE: Well, Dad _____ a piece of cake when he _____ into something hard. (*eat/bite*)
WOMAN: And it was my ring?!
ALICE: Yes. I guess it _____ off your finger while you _____ the cake this morning. (*fall/make*)

IV. NEGATIVES

A. In English you use only one negative in a sentence.
Some negatives don't have *no* or *not* in them. They don't look like negatives, but they are.
1. *Seldom* = not too often
2. *Rarely* = not usually
3. *Never* = not ever

Examples: 1. *He seldom eats fish.* (He doesn't often eat fish.)
2. *He rarely eats fish.* (He doesn't usually eat fish.)
3. *He never eats fish.* (He doesn't ever eat fish.)

B. Fill in the blanks. Follow the example below.

Example: Doesn't he *ever* study?
—No, *never.*
I don't believe it.
—Really. He *never* studies.

1. _____ you _____ eat at home?
—No, _____. We always go to restaurants.
Every day?
—Yes. We _____ eat at home.

2. _____ he _____ leave the shop?
—No, _____.
That's hard to believe.
—It's true. He _____ leaves the shop.

3. _____ you _____ save any money?
—No, _____.
You must be joking.
—No, I'm not. I _____ save a penny.

4. _____ Pedro _____ think about his old girlfriends?
—No, _____.
That's strange.
—Yes, it is. Pedro lives in the present. He _____ thinks about the past.

Irregular Verbs

I. BASE FORM and PAST FORM are the same.

BASE	PAST
bet	bet
cost	cost
cut	cut
hit	hit
hurt	hurt
knit	knit
let	let
put	put
quit	quit
read	read*
rid	rid
set	set
shut	shut
split	split
spread	spread

II. BASE FORM and PAST FORM are different.

BASE	PAST	BASE	PAST
bend	bent	feel	felt
build	built	keep	kept
lend	lent	leave	left
send	sent	mean	meant
spend	spent	sleep	slept
bleed	bled	hang	hung
feed	fed	stick	stuck
hold	held	win	won
lead	led		
meet	met		

*pronounced "red."

BASE	PAST	BASE	PAST
bring	brought	steal	stole
buy	bought	wake	woke
fight	fought		*or* waked
think	thought		
catch	caught	tear	tore
teach	taught	wear	wore
find	found	grow	grew
		know	knew
		throw	threw
take	took		
		bite	bit
get	got	hide	hid
lose	lost		
shine	shone	take	took
	or shined		
shoot	shot	drive	drove
sell	sold	ride	rode
tell	told	write	wrote
become	became	begin	began
come	came	drink	drank
run	ran	ring	rang
		sing	sang
have	had	swim	swam
hear	heard		
make	made	eat	ate
pay	paid	fall	fell
say	said	do	did
sit	sat	draw	drew
stand	stood	fly	flew
		forget	forgot
break	broke	give	gave
choose	chose	go	went
freeze	froze	lie	lay
speak	spoke	see	saw

NEW ENGLISH 900

THE INTONATION LINES

The next ten pages contain the 150 Base Sentences found in this book. They are arranged by unit. The sentences are not accompanied by the context in which they appear in the actual lessons.

The blue lines that appear with a sentence indicate how it is spoken in American English. If you look at the lines you will be able to recognize the basic intonation patterns of English. The language employs three pitches: low, medium, and high.

Example: How are you?
high
medium
low

The intonation lines should not be used independently, but should be studied along with the sentences as they are spoken, either by your teacher or on the tapes that accompany the book. It is not really possible to learn how to produce a sound by studying only a printed representation of that sound. As you repeat the sentences aloud after your teacher or after the tapes, you will gradually become familiar with the intonation patterns and learn how to use them.

301 I resigned.

302 You liked the job, didn't you?

303 But it was an interesting job, wasn't it?

304 We handled all the advertising and promotion for the Fair.

305 I type sixty words a minute.

306 No, not today.

307 But did you look in the newspaper?

308 Did you check with them?

309 No, I didn't.

310 Why not?

311 You need recommendations to get a good job.

312 Mr. Crawford is difficult to work for, right?

313 Is that possible?

314 Maybe you're his seventh secretary in two years!

315 Don't mention it.

316 Some of these pictures could be in magazines.

317 You had a mustache!

318 You're standing with a guy with long blond hair.

319 He looks American.

320 I met him at the art school downtown.

321 He was in love with this woman.

322 She didn't love Michael anymore.

323 She fell in love with me.

324 Just like that?

325 Well, sure, I flirted with her, but I flirt with everyone!

326 You know I can't resist a pretty face.

327 He never spoke to me again.

328 About a year ago I tried to call him, but he hung up on me.

329 We saw each other a few times.

330 Things like that don't last long.

331 There is so much to tell you, Mama.

332 At 7:00 the alarm clock rang and woke us up.

333 Even the water tastes different!

334 At 9:00 I left the house.

335 At night, after dinner, we talked and watched television.

336 At about 9:30 one of Pedro's friends stopped in to say "hello."

337 At about 11:00 Pedro called each one of his twenty girlfriends to say good night and told each one a different story.

338 I like Pedro more and more.

339 Yesterday, I learned the word "embarrassed."

340 She lives upstairs.

341 My father died the year I was born.

342 It broke my mother's heart to leave, but it also broke her heart to stay.

343 She sold her diamond ring, the only thing she had, and bought two tickets to Mexico.

344 After all, I was only a child.

345 But our new life was not like my mother's golden dreams.

346 I grew up and had to go to work.

347 He had a little money, and I spent a few happy years with him.

348 I got new clothes and lived in a fine house.

349 But I didn't love him, and I think he knew it, too.

350 We fought about it and made each other miserable.

351 He is just like you, so sensible, maybe too sensible.

352 Joana is growing up before my eyes.

353 Every day she grows more mature, less shy, and more confident.

354 She's getting serious about art again, so she's going to take some courses at one of the schools here.

355 She's talented, but not very patient.

356 I am enjoying the Fair, but most of all, I am enjoying the children.

357 At first, Joana was nervous about her English, but now she is almost fluent.

358 So, my dear, how are you?

359 How are things at home?

360 I read and reread all your letters.

361   What are we going to do with Ali?

362   He'll be seven in a few weeks.

363   It's time to think about his future.

364   You spoil him, Zahra.

365   Why can't Ali be more like Hussein?

366   They'll never behave the same way.

367   We take him to the Fair, and what does he do?

368   You can't make excuses for him forever.

369   Last year he misbehaved because he didn't understand English.

370   This year you won't be able to use that excuse.

371   He won't listen to anybody.

372   I'll look for a school for creative children.

373   Won't you ever believe me?

374   But next year, back in Iran, things will be different.

375   Ali will make you proud one day.

376 Wouldn't you like to take a walk to the Fair today?

377 There won't be many people there at this hour.

378 i'd rather go on a weekday.

379 Take a one-day vacation.

380 People come from around the world to see the Fair.

381 You live right around the corner.

382 What's the weather like today?

383 It's a beautiful spring day.

384 It would be good for you to spend a day in the sun.

385 Can I get to the Fair by bus?

386 It goes right to the Fair.

387 Where is my good coat?

388 The sun is shining, and it's going to get warm.

389 Are you sure it's not going to rain?

390 I don't think so, but anything is possible.

391   We'd like your agency to handle the publicity.

392   Now let me make sure I have all the facts.

393   Yes, and by the way, the Pavilion will display many of the entries during the final month of the competition.

394   Now, the entries must all be oil paintings, correct?

395   Is there an age limit for the participants?

396   We were thinking of thirty or thirty-five.

397   But you must know more about this than I do.

398   Where were we?

399   What kind of a grant were you thinking of?

400   We were going to offer a scholarship, a living allowance, and air fare to and from Brazil.

401   What about the deadline for the entries.

402   Six months from today?

403   They have to enter by November 1.

404   We'll announce the winner the following month.

405   Well, I can have sample brochures ready for you in a week.

406 As you see, Claire, the office is very formal.

407 Yes, I realized that when Mr. Crawford interviewed me.

408 We keep our files in alphabetical order.

409 He comes in once a month and goes over the books.

410 May I ask why you're leaving?

411 I'd rather not say.

412 Well, we keep the office supplies in this cabinet—paper,
typewriter ribbons, pads, pencils, pens, envelopes, etc.

413 Do you have any questions so far?

414 How often do you work late?

415 Hardly ever.

416 Because I don't know if I can stay late.

417 When I was a girl, I wanted to be a lawyer.

418 It must be difficult to work while you're going to school.

419 His office is across the hall.

420 He gets angry when you're late.

421 You have to continue your studies or you'll never find a good job.

422 We don't even know who she is

423 Is she from a good family?

424 Can you tell me what her father does?

425 You don't know how important you are to us.

426 They have a daughter, a very pretty girl.

427 She's just about your age.

428 They won't recognize you, of course, but they'll remember us, and they'll be very happy to see you.

429 I worry about you, and I suppose I always will.

430 P.S. Write soon.   **431** It was a warm day, warm for April.

432 People were walking around the Fair with their coats over their arms.

433 The sun was bright, and there were little white clouds in the blue sky.

434 A thousand vendors were selling ice cream, hot dogs, and cold drinks.

435 It was a beautiful, spring morning—the kind you want to last forever.

436 Later in the afternoon, the sun was not so bright, the sky not so blue.

437 The little white clouds were now large and gray.

438 There was a drop here, a drop there . . . then ten thousand noisy drops.

439 People shouted and ran in every direction.

440 Then there was silence, the sun, the blue sky, and a rainbow.

441 She knows where she's going and what she wants, and she's willing to work for it.

442 When I married my husband, I quit.

443 After I left him, I went back to the same office.

444 When I came here, I got a job right away.

445 I was happy with anything.

446 First things first.   447 I can run an office.

448 Uh . . . There must be more.

449 Well, then, if you can do all that, you don't have to work for the Mr. Crawfords of the world.

450 Well, what kind of job would you like?

NEW ENGLISH 900

WORD INDEX

On the following pages you will find a list of the words that appear in this book. They are arranged in alphabetical order. Each word is followed by a sentence.

like   I don't like dinner parties.

This is the sentence in which the word first appears in context in the book. Following the sentence, two numbers are given.

our   Are those students in our class?   3/1

These numbers indicate the unit and lesson in which the word and sentence appear. That is, 5/2 means Unit Five, Lesson Two.

Nouns are listed under the singular form, even if in the book they appeared in the plural.

friend   Where are my friends?

Verbs are listed under the base form.

wait   I'm sorry to keep you waiting.

The only exceptions to the above are irregular forms.

was   I was in the bathroom.

Phrases, idioms, and other units of meaning that consist of more than one word are listed separately.

good morning   Good morning, sir.

This index is not intended to be a substitute for a dictionary, but you will often be able to understand a word from the sentence given with it. You can also refer back to the particular unit and lesson to study the word in a larger context.

drop	There was a drop here, a drop there, then ten thousand noisy drops. 26/2
drove	She drove a small car. 20/2
during	Yes, and by the way, the Pavilion will display many of the entries during the final month of the competition. 24/1
earn	I earn $180 a week. 19/1
earth	People come from the four corners of the earth to see the Fair. 23/1
editor	Henry Leeds is the editor. 25/2
education	You need an education to get a good job. 19/2
embarrass	It could be embarrassing. 20/2
employee	Claire doesn't know how Mr. Crawford treats his employees. 25/1
employment	Didn't you *stop in* at the employment office? 19/1
empty	The office is empty. 24/1
engage	Michael was engaged to this woman. 20/2
enjoy	I won't enjoy my dinner without you. 22/2
enter	They have to enter by November 1. 24/2
entry	Yes, and by the way, the Pavilion will display may of the entries during the final month of the competition. 24/1
envelope	Well, we keep the office supplies in this cabinet—paper, typewriter ribbons, pads, pencils, pens, envelopes, etc. 25/1
even	Even the water tastes different! 21/1
everywhere	People come from everywhere to see the Fair. 23/1
exam	It must be difficult to work while you are studying for exams. 25/2
exciting	It was an exciting job, wasn't it? 19/1
excuse	You can't make excuses for him forever. 22/1
exhibition	Some of these pictures could be in an exhibition. 20/1
expect	He expected to marry her. 20/2
experience	You have more experience. 24/1
explain	Can you explain why Laura quit? 25/1
fact	Now let me make sure I have all the facts. 24/1
fall	Fall is my favorite season. 23/2
far	People come from far and wide to see the Fair. 23/1
fare	We were going to offer a scholarship, a living allowance, and air fare to and from Brazil. 24/2
farm	Back on the farm, things will be different. 22/2
fascinating	It was a fascinating job, wasn't it? 19/1
fell	She fell in love with me. 20/2
figure	You know I can't resist a nice figure. 20/2
file	Claire doesn't know where the newsletter file is. 25/1
final	Yes, and by the way, the Pavilion will display many of the entries during the final month of the competition. 24/1
finally	Finally we got a divorce. 21/2
fire	Didn't Mr. Crawford fire Laura? 19/2

part	We will display many of the entries during last part of the competition. 24/1
participant	Is there an age limit for the participants? 24/1
pay check	Did you *pick up* your pay check? 19/2
personnel	We keep the forms, insurance, personnel, etc. in this cabinet 25/1
photograph	You asked for a photograph. 21/1
photography	Some of these pictures could be in a photography show. 20/1
picture	Hey, here's an old picture of you. 20/1
plan	And that, Mr. Crawford, is our plan. 24/1
plan	He planned to marry her. 20/2
plant	I was planting them. 24/2
point	Do you have any questions at this point? 25/2
position	I accepted a new position this morning. 19/1
possibility	I never thought about other possibilities. 26/3
possible	Is that possible? 19/2
praise	You praise him. 22/1
problem	Business problems don't last a long time. 20/2
promotion	We handled all the advertising and promotion for the Fair. 19/1
proud	I am very proud of them. 21/3
publicity	We'd like your agency to handle the publicity. 24/1
publish	We'd like your office to publish the newsletter. 24/1
question	Laura, may I ask you a question? 25/1
radio	I turned on the radio, and we listened to the news. 21/1
rain	Are you sure it's not going to rain? 23/2
rainbow	Then there was silence, the sun, the blue sky, and a rainbow. 26/2
raise	I asked for a raise this morning. 19/1
ran	I ran into her at the art school downtown. 20/1
rang	At 7:00 the alarm clock rang and woke us up. 21/1
rather	I'd rather go on a weekday. 23/1
real	He doesn't have any real friends here. 21/3
realize	Yes, I realized that when Mr. Crawford inteviewed me. 25/1
reason	And there was no reason to stay in Barcelona. 21/2
recognize	They won't recognize you, of course, but they'll remember us, and they'll be very happy to see you. 26/1
recommendation	Mr. Crawford isn't going to give me a recommendation. 19/2
reference	I realized that when he asked me for three references. 25/1
remember	Because I didn't remember your number. 19/2
resist	You know I can't resist a pretty face. 20/2
ribbon	Well, we keep the office supplies in this cabinet—paper, typewriter ribbons, pads, pencils, pens, envelopes, etc. 25/1

ring	She sold her diamond ring, the only thing she had, and bought two tickets to Mexico. 21/2
romance	School romances don't last a long time. 20/2
rub	I was rubbing my eyes. 24/2
ruin	I ruin his dinner. 22/2
rule	We were discussing the rules of the competition. 24/1
run	I run a mile a day. 19/1
run away	He runs away! 22/1
said	No, I never said anything to him again. 20/2
sample	I'll have the samples ready in a week. 24/2
saw	I saw you at the art school downtown. 20/1
scholarship	We were going to offer a scholarship, a living allowance, and air fare to and from Brazil. 24/2
science	We were going to take a science course, but we changed our minds. 24/2
season	Spring is my favorite season. 23/2
secret	He likes secrets. 22/1
seem	Everything here seems different, but, at the same time, everything seems the same. 21/1
sell	Where did you sell your pictures? 20/1
semester	Three or four times a semester. 25/2
sent	I sent her a card. 20/2
separate	Michael was separated from this woman. 20/2
shine	The sun is shining, and it's going to get warm. 23/2
ship	Can I get there by ship? 23/2
shook	I realized that when he shook my hand. 25/1
shorthand	Oh, yes, I type and take shorthand in two languages. 26/3
shout	People shouted and ran in every direction. 26/2
shy	Every day she grows more mature, less shy, and more confident. 21/3
silence	Then there was silence, the sun, the blue sky, and a rainbow. 26/2
skill	You need skills to get a good job. 19/2
sleep	I wasn't sleeping. 24/2
slob	You're a slob, Pedro, but you're a great photographer. 20/1
snack	We keep the snacks, cookies, fruit, etc. in this cabinet 25/1
snow	Are you sure it's not going to snow? 23/2
sold	I sold them at the art school downtown. 20/1
speech	Must you make a speech at the meeting? 24/1
spent	He had a little money, and I spent a few happy years with him. 21/2
spoke	He never spoke to me again. 20/2
spring	It's a beautiful spring day. 23/2
start	When will you start to look for a school for him? 22/2
station	The number 20 bus goes right to the station. 23/2
stranger	You mustn't talk to strangers. 24/1